The Changing Landscape

The Changing Landscape

SALISBURY, CONNECTICUT

CHRISTOPHER RAND

New York • OXFORD UNIVERSITY PRESS • 1 9 6 8

TO MY FAMILY

THESE ESSAYS have been written over a long period, from 1952 to 1966, and I have altered them very little here. Thus a few of the situations described are out of date: some of the farming changes mentioned in 1952, for instance, have been superseded by later ones, such as the adoption of pole-barns for cattle. I have not tried to catch up with these new developments. Nor have I tried to show consistency in my own attitude throughout. In 1952 I was almost offended by the changes in Salisbury, but by 1966 I had come to see change itself as an enduring, reliable quality in the town; and I hope readers won't be disturbed by the difference. Finally, the essays sometimes overlap: a change in some aspect of the landscape is noted sligthly in an early essay, then explored at more length in a later one. I hope readers won't be disturbed by this either; it merely reflects the learning process.

C.R.

Acknowledgments

THIS WHOLE WORK was undertaken by *The New Yorker* and me together, and without *The New Yorker* it could not have been done. I have also been helped by innumerable friends in Salisbury and elsewhere. I cannot list them—nor would they all want me to—but they know what they did for me, and I trust they know how thankful I am.

C.R.

Contents

The Changing Landscape

I. THE FARMING

FOR A FEW YEARS now I have seen change and decay attack the countryside where I grew up, around Salisbury, in northwest Connecticut. I spent my boyhood holidays in Salisbury; I was in my teens here in the 1920s, and in the early 'thirties I worked a few summers here on my father's farm. Out of those years I got a picture of stable country life—with cows, horses, men, and crops following their rounds unswervingly—that stayed with me for the decade till the war's end, a time I spent mainly in California and Asia. When I came back briefly after VJ-Day, though, I began to notice things going off the track. The most striking of them then was the abandonment, to brush, of rocky or hilly meadows, with which our part of Connecticut was well endowed. Though hard to work, such fields had been in nearly every landscape —open spaces on the walks from certain points to certain other points—and to me they had seemed as timeless as the hills. Now they were mowed no longer and were going first into weeds, then into sumac and birch. The change was gloomily plain if you walked much, because second growth is so nasty to get through, and I hardly escaped it for a day of that visit. I also learned, then and on later trips, that berry-picking had nearly ended in our region, and that hay-cocks or oat-shocks were rarely to be seen in summer fields any more. My awakening kept on intermittently till this fall, when I came back for a longer visit than usual and was told that bobolinks had left their good lowland meadows and that the shape of barn roofs was starting to change, all because of new farming ways.

At this time a dairying neighbor, George Miner, told me there was no team of work-horses left nearer than the south side of Canaan Mountain, which is perhaps five miles from his farm. Later my brother Jake, also a dairyman, said that this was wrong—that he himself knew of a team just over the state line in Millerton, New York, which would be some two miles closer. Further study has led Mr. Miner to change his figures, and he now reports two teams of horses and one of mules within reasonable distance. Even so the change is great from before the war, when there must have been two, three, or more teams for every square mile of Salisbury township (apart, that is, from the Taconic Mountains). As I heard these tidings I brooded on the revolution they bespoke, and so I decided to look into it, right down to the bobolinks.

We are a dairying country, raising milk for New York, the Connecticut cities, and several boarding schools in our midst, a duty that entails two main jobs —the direct care of cows and the growing of their food. Both jobs have been shaken by the revolution, an event whose chief elements, so far as I can learn, are the spread of knowledge, the rise of the machine, and the near-disappearance of hand labor. In the food-raising job most of the changes can be linked sooner or later to a new technique called grassland farming. When I was a boy the farmers here would grow at least four crops each year—corn, oats, clover, and timothy hay—all different in their nature and standing in separate fields; besides which other fields were set apart for pasture; and this variety, with its contrasts of greens and yellows, changing as the summer went on, made the old patchwork of farm landscape. Nowadays, I hear from the neighbors and see partly with my eyes, the patchwork is starting to blur, its lines getting erased by a tendency to plant all acreage to the same crop: a heavy lush mixture of grasses, dominated as a rule by something called Ladino clover, that can be mowed as hay, or chopped for silage, or grazed right off by cows as pasture. The mixture has already gone far to drive out timothy, which used to put the light gray-green in July fields; and corn, it seems, is next. My brother, who started a small farm in 1946, has never had a cornfield or silo on it, though he says this would have been out of the question as late as the mid-'thirties. He makes up the lack through better hay and through buying modern extras like beet-pulp. Separate pastures have dwindled too. "The whole idea now," Jake tells me, "is to get the most milk per acre, so you don't use poor fields or distant fields any more."

The rich new grasslands yield three crops a year, and often the cows are turned right onto the second and third of these. They are apt to be grazed on small patches at a time, to which they are kept by movable electric fences, a big difference from ten years ago; then cows were turned daily through the summer into the same large fixed expanse, and it was used for nothing else. There was a contrast in texture between hayfields and pastures. Hayfields after mowing were stubbly but even.

Pastures were more closely and smoothly cropped, down to a fraction of an inch in places, but they always had bumps left in them, perhaps of thistles or milkweed. It was rather like the difference between plush laid on a flat surface and velvet on a lumpy one. Now the contrast is fading, and in among the stubble one finds low mats of vegetation, almost like moss; one finds rich red clover blossoms, plainly cultivated, side by side with hoof-marks and manure; all signifying that the cows have been in the hay, a state of affairs once thought intolerable. And behind these scenes a sketchy electric fence will run, on its spindly impermanent stakes, a sign of flux and the withering of barriers.

When chopped for silage the new grass blend needs little or no curing in the field, so it can be got in quickly, without fear of the early summer rains that of old would delay us by wetting half-cured hay, forcing it to be turned out for more curing, then wetting it again. The haying of my day began in late June and dragged on all summer, broken only by the need to cultivate corn a few times with the horses, and later to get the oats in, an August job. Now haying starts by the end of May and is over, so far as the first cutting goes, by July Fourth. Many farmers in our neighborhood take a two-week vacation in July or August, a habit that would have seemed preposterous in my boyhood, when I used to pray secretly for midsummer rains, the only thing that could bring cease from toil.

These vacations are in line with one of the revolution's main features: a tendency for dirt farmers to become like city technicians or white-collar folk. The paper-work for anyone running a farm has swollen to ugly dimensions, because of new techniques that must be studied and be-

cause costs and production are watched with an alertness
undreamt of before. "Half the pleasure has gone out of
farming," my brother says, "because you have to watch
your expenses so." The above-named George Miner says
it has all gone out.

These men view life in a classical New England way,
without rose-colored glasses, yet even so I think they
have a point. From what I have seen, I believe farmers
are suffering as cruelly as anyone from the plague of
mimeographed "literature." As for hired hands, they
have turned into mechanics because of the fancy gear
they handle. I heard of one machine the other day with
122 points that must be greased. The man who runs
such a thing no longer pitches hay—no one pitches hay
now—and he has the same rights as a factory hand because he knows he can be one if he chooses, in the Connecticut war plants. He has set days off, and it is the
boss's hard luck if no one is around then to milk the cows.
In the summer he goes on daylight time, which was not
allowed in my boyhood; when the day starts that early
an hour is often lost while the dew burns off the fields,
and so standard time ("God's time") was the rule with
us. Hired men are paid well now, and if married they
expect houses with kitchen gadgets. George Miner was
explaining this to me one evening, and I asked if farmers
still filled their men's cellars with potatoes in the fall, a
bounden duty in my time. "Oh, farm hands don't eat
potatoes any more," he said. "They eat potato chips."
George does not spoil a story, but one cannot say he is
wrong about this. I know of a hand in town whose wife,
according to Dame Rumor, feeds him nothing but a
breakfast food called Cheerios. He was seen preparing a
garden not long ago, and his mother-in-law asked him if

he was going to plant Cheerios in it. The older generation gets many laughs from the younger here now.

The machine has crept in to a point where the Miner farm, a modest enough one with 25 milking cows, has 68 rubber tires on it (ten years ago there were four). George was recently offered a "fleet rate" by a Millerton tire dealer. Apart from trucks and tractors, the 68 tires are on things like a wagon, a manure-spreader, a hay-rake, and a plough. With the switch to rubber, farm life has sped up giddily. Manure piles—once a stable form of wealth here—can rarely be found now, as the sweepings of most barns are put right in the spreader each morning and whisked to a distant field. One neighbor heard a comparison on the radio awhile back: if a farmer ten years ago had a team and two thousand dollars' worth of machinery, he would now have no team and five thousand dollars' worth, this fast getting obsolete. Farmers I have asked say this is near the truth.

My brother has a comparison also: his two men, with a truck and wagon, can get hay in as fast now as eight or nine men with three teams of horses could do it fifteen years ago on my father's farm. That farm was a big one, inefficiently spread out by modern standards. When haying we would keep two or three men at the barn, working in the loft, and two or three in the field, bunching up hay-cocks and pitching onto wagons. The three wagons, each with a teamster, would lumber back and forth, sometimes needing half an hour for a one-way trip (when empty they joggled so on their iron-shod wheels that I imagine they traveled as far up and down as forward). Now my brother's two men and truck and wagon whizz out to the field, load up, whizz back and unload, all in unison. I know of one farmer who is working an-

other man's fields a couple of miles from his place by
state highway; the trip is no real hindrance now. Farmers have loading machines to help them, and the hay,
when not chopped, is baled—my aunt says it looks like
lumps of sugar in the fields. In former times oats were
mowed and tied in bundles by a machine called a reaper
and binder; then the bundles were stacked in shocks to
cure a few days before threshing. Now the oats are left
standing till the last minute of ripeness, then mowed by
a combine, which threshes and drops the grain and straw
as it rolls along. That is why there are so few hay-cocks
and straw-shocks nowadays.

The new grass silage, my brother says, is so heavy,
from its lushness and uncured state, that men and horses
couldn't handle it—pitch it or draw a loader to load it.
He says machines have been brought to where they can
do a pretty clean job on crops now, but they don't approach the refinement of human care in the old days. We
took pride in hand-mowing the edges of fields—with
scythes—and the nasty places round rocks and trees that
a mowing machine couldn't reach. This was a job to be
done after the main haying, or on off days when hay was
wet, and it was one of the things that made the season
long. From a strict economic view it was a luxury, in a
class with keeping barns freshly painted, yet it gave the
countryside a well-groomed look that satisfied us, I believe. Now when you walk through a field you may see
a fringe of tall straggly dead grass round its edge, or
patches of such grass in the middle in the rough places.
The grass has an old brown color. It would be foolish to
complain about this, yet it must be noted down.

In some places, my brother says, heavy earth-moving
gear is being used to take out rocks, or bulldoze the brush

off brush-lots, or even bury stone walls so the planting
and harvesting machines can get a longer run. This behavior leaves scars on the land, of course. But a farmer
must be rich to indulge in it, and there are few such
around Salisbury so far.

The change in barn roofs, which has only begun but
which Jake feels will continue, stems from the new haying methods, chiefly the baling. Between the two wars
nearly all up-to-date barns in our country had high gambrel roofs, which would take a hayfork on an overhead
track. There were two kinds of forks, the grappling type,
which had big opposed claws, and the harpoon type,
with two prongs for stabbing straight down into hay,
and little trippable barbs for keeping them there. The
load was driven up against the barn's end, the fork was
stuck into it, and with much screaming and groaning of
pulleys a mass of hay was raised to the big loft door, outside which it paused a moment and then moved on and
vanished in the darkness. Not everyone knew what happened in that darkness, but I did. A crew of two or three
hands, perhaps including myself, was inside waiting.
The fork would rumble in, hung from steel wheels on
the steel track. When it got where we wanted we would
shout in unison, and then, though often not at once, the
ropes would be stopped from without and the fork
tripped. The hay would drop ponderously amid floating
dust, and we would pull it apart with forks and stow it
in the sides. There was an art to filling a loft this way—
as there was to laying a hayload—and good men could
pack a fearful amount in by summer's end. But now with
the baling of hay the art isn't needed, and, my brother
says, the bales themselves, being heavy, are hard to lug
around in that space. His new barn has a small loft a

truck can drive into, via a ramp at the back, and that way the bales roll off neatly. Other farms keep bales in ground-level sheds near the barn. Gambrel roofs, Jake says, are "getting to be a thing of the past," a phrase he uses often. He says a type of barn once popular in this neighborhood, then obsolete, has gotten useful again. This is a small one with a passage right through the middle, usually the short way, which you can drive a hayload into. From it the hay can be pitched by hand into bays on either side, and mechanical forks aren't needed. There were many such barns when I was a boy, most of them used only as a last resort in a big harvest. They were built well, with hand-shaped timbers, they had a musty smell of old hay, and the low walls of the bays had often been polished by loads brushing past in the years. We liked playing in them but didn't take them seriously as a part of farm life. Now they are handy for trucks and bales. The barn, having swollen, is shrinking.

Cows themselves, in the words of George Miner, are so damn high-toned now it's awful. "They're particular as hell," he says. "You have to cater to them all the time. Have to curry them. Wash their tails. You remember we didn't bother with them too much in the old days. Now if you try to make a living off cows you've got to be with them all the time. Scratch their necks. 'Cater to them' is the only way I can put it."

Jake agrees. He says cows are tamer and get closer attention, especially as youngstock, than before. In our boyhood cows ready to calve might on occasion be turned out on a wild expanse called Butterly behind my father's farm—one or two hundred acres of hilly woodland opening now and then into pasture. They would have their calves and would often run wild with them. Afterward they would tend to jump fences, kick over pails, and otherwise play jokes—become "characters" in the sense now used of humans. Such cows don't get by today, Jake says. To give much milk, it has been established, cows must be well in hand. So they are usually turned out in small fields near by, often of the new grassland clover, or sometimes of "improved" pasture—fertilized, that is, and with the weeds mowed off. Youngstock that are still in the old rough lots are given salt inside the near fence, so they can be checked on daily, and petted and led to nuzzle. Calves in pasture are fed grain, a new thing. Jake says the feet of his cattle must be trimmed more often now than of old because they don't wear down so fast. He says cows puff more when going up hills.

In our day pastures were far off because cows could walk to them if they had to. Meadows were close because wagons were slow. Now the idea is to reverse this. Lester Simonton, one of the best dairymen in our town, who of old would ride a horse to get the cows sometimes, now tries to arrange it so they eat their fill and lie down with their cud an hour after leaving the barn. (He uses electric fences a lot. He says grown cows get broken to them, so that half the time the current can be left off, but this doesn't work with young stock.)

Cows' valuations and output of milk have shot up along with everything. Twenty years ago a good grade cow (not purebred, that is) would cost seventy-five dollars in these parts. Now it would be four or five hundred. The cow, viewed as a unit, puts out a third or a half more milk than it used to, from better breeding, feeding, and care. My brother has 18 milking cows, and they give more than half as much as the 45 at my father's did. The cash income is about the same because of high prices. My brother pays two men where my father paid at least five, but says he is making no more profit. (Farmers here talk poor now as always.)

George Miner thinks cows get tired of the fancy stuff they are fed today—this includes, according to him, all kinds of pellet feeds and everything under the sun, moon, and stars. "They hanker for some of that old kind of grass," he says. "They like variety. You know when you go out to a restaurant you will go now to an Italian one, now to a Swedish one, and so on. It's the same with cows. Sometimes when you mow a pasture, and cut off the old dead tops of weeds, the cows will come in and eat their fill of tender green grass. And then just for the heck of it they will pick up some of the old dry cut stuff and lie down and chew it."

One day after hearing all this I went up on Butterly, which I had known as a child, to see what it looked like. Cows hadn't been grazed there since the 'thirties, Jake said. Butterly is chiefly woodland, as noted above, but it once had many old clearings in grass, and worn paths leading through it here and there. Now, I found, the paths were choked. I almost lost one of them—it had been of trodden dirt with grass on either side—in a thicket of birch and sumac ten feet high. Another had briers arched over it so I could hardly tear through. I kept making detours. I visited one place where formerly you could walk freely, or even turn somersaults, on the short grass, but now I had to breast my way. Forests of goldenrod and sumac were standing there, the goldenrod up to my neck. The ground itself was mostly bare but for dead leaves and dead bits of stalk, though small grass patches here and there fought this litter and the shade. In the woods some glades still functioned dimly, though with much dead grass from no grazing. Green carpets had become brown carpets of leaves, and I flushed a partridge from a spot that of old wouldn't hide a mouse.

Yet in woods nearby that had always been woods— within my memory, that is—the change was not striking. Old paths under hemlocks were almost the same after twenty years. I suppose a status quo, different from the chaos of neglected meadows, had been enforced by the trees and their shade. Jake told me of one change in the woods, though. In our boyhood most large woodland stretches were visited at times by traveling sawmills, which would set up for a few months, cut timber, saw it, and withdraw, leaving great mounds of sawdust in the wilds. This is getting to be a thing of the past, Jake says. He says a few sawmill men who are behind the times still work that way—go in with a couple of pairs of horses and put up a rough timber shack and spend the winter there. But it is disappearing. The modern operator goes in with big things like bulldozers, mechanical saws, and caterpillar tractors. These slap trees around in dinosaur style and feed them onto trucks, which take them elsewhere for processing. It lessens the intercourse of man and nature, but I can't say what it does to the woods as I haven't yet come on any so treated. The main scars I have seen in the woods are still those of the chestnut blight and the great hurricane of 1938.*

The lady who told me of the bobolinks had formerly owned some flat meadows by the Housatonic. Much of these had been in grass, and the bobolinks had been all

* For more about the changing woods, see Chapter IV.

through them in the season. Now, she told me, they had gone away because of some changes in the farming, and she referred me to an adjacent naturalist, Lincoln Foster, for details. He enlightened me in short order. Bobolinks nest in the grass and their season begins in May, he said; fledglings are not on their own till mid-June. With the advancement of the haying season there has been much disturbance, and perhaps slaughter, of bobolinks by machines, and the former have left the good bottom meadows for the abandoned upland ones. This change has coincided, by the way, with one in the winter or Southern part of the bobolinks' year. Bobolinks stay in rice in the South, along the Atlantic seaboard, and are known there as rice-birds. But of late much rice production has moved away to the Gulf and the West Coast, and the bobolinks haven't followed it. Their feeding grounds have thus been restricted and they have been concentrated at the mercy of hunters—they are deemed fair game in parts of the South. They are having a hard time all round, in short, or so Mr. Foster says.

He says too that nighthawks and whippoorwills have been affected by the change here. These birds lay their eggs (without nests) on open rocky ledges—that is to say in the kind of field now being abandoned. Yet they come in on a low glide and don't like the obstruction of second growth. It is driving them from the countryside, Mr. Foster says, and they are taking to the flat roofs of secondary Northeastern cities like Albany. He says deer are having it easy now and are plentiful, because saplings and seedlings are their dish; but a day of reckoning may be in store when the abandoned land grows up, as they find less to eat in mature forests. Pileated woodpeckers, on the other hand, are thought to have no such problem.

The more the forest, the better they do; they are on the wax now and expected to continue.

My cousin Sam Ferguson, a trout fisherman, says the vogue of asphalt roads has changed his sport. Roads often run along streams, of course. Sam's point is that in the old days a shower would quickly rile many streams with run-off from the dirt, but this no longer happens because of the asphalt. Riled water is prized by fishermen here as elsewhere because their quarry is thought to be on the *qui vive* in it, looking for worms and other things to wash their way. Traditionally fishermen get in the stream as fast as they can after a storm. Sam says they do it no longer. Of course he is a fisherman himself,* and we know of them and their veracity.

I can add something about asphalt roads. They put out a strong smell, and when you walk on them many smells of woods and fields are drowned. Life has more variety on dirt roads, it seems, and we must have lost dozens of them here in twenty years.

There are the apple trees. Many places here have old orchards—a few trees planted for family rather than commercial use—but they hardly bear at all now. So many blights have settled on us, perhaps from increased travel, that apples must be sprayed eight or more times a year to be fruitful. Life is too short for the owners to do this, or so they think, and the cost of hiring a spray man is forbidding. So trees are neglected and few new ones planted. There is a preponderance of the older genera- tion among them; the typical Salisbury tree is gnarled and cranky, shot through with woodpecker holes. Often these old trees have new branches shooting upward from

* He is deceased by now, God rest his soul.

their tops. I suppose they were pruned fairly well till a few years back and then let go, and a rush of young life has followed. The new branches reach for the sky like unruly pompadours.

Having orchards outside, the houses had apple barrels within; but no longer. The good apple days were in my early childhood, and I have been checking on them by consulting an older neighbor, Phil Warner, whose family's cellar was always well stocked then. He saws they would start eating Northern Spies in the fall, then Baldwins, then Russets, and this would take them into May. In July the Astrakhans ripened, the first of the new crop, so there were only two months a year without apples of some kind. Trees took care of themselves then; the Warner family had an orchard on Butterly that got no attention, except for picking, and that produced well year after year till the mid-'thirties. The old cellars were better for storing apples, too, because furnaces are hard on them and so are the cement floors that are laid under houses now.

There was cider in the cellars too. We have our share of puritanism here, but for some reason it was thought right to drink hard cider almost any time. Phil Warner suspects the cider was looked on as a food, not an intoxicant, though he thinks this was misleading. Anyway, if a farmer called on another when I was a boy, morning, noon, or night, there was apt to be a parade to the cool cellar, and a pitcher drawn from the cider-smelling keg and glasses raised all round. If a boy was along he had his glass with the rest. A farmer who dealt much with others might drink a half gallon a day this way, whether at home or abroad, and some think the New England character got its flavor from the cider taste, rather than any weaning on pickles. But hearty cider-drinking is a thing of the past now, in Salisbury at least—not getting to be that way, but gotten. You can still buy cider or apples, but it isn't easy, and few people do it on the barrel scale.

Of humans the great vanished race with us is the teamsters. In my boyhood teamsters grew locally or came down from the north, from Maine, New Hampshire, and Vermont, where wages were lower. These latter men were close to nature and could do things like carve good axe handles, better than you could buy. As a rule teamsters did a vast amount of work in a day, but at a slow, lasting pace. They went step by step. One afternoon I was working in the hayloft with a teamster, a portly Maine man, temporarily detached from his horses. I used to chew tobacco then—it was a manly way to take on nicotine without burning the barn down—and I got out my plug and offered him some as I knew he liked it. He thanked me but said he thought he wouldn't take any right then. He had had some greens for lunch, he said, and had put a great deal of salt on them ("greddeal" of salt was the way he pronounced it). This had made him thirsty and dry, and so he had taken his teeth out, and he didn't think he would chew for the present, though he might later. The whole response took time, and as he spoke he stowed big forkfuls of hay under the roof-beams, slowly and methodically. And slowly and methodically he went on with us for ten years, occasionally having trouble with his back, but now he has disappeared and neither Jake nor I know where he is.

Teamsters got up early, though not so early as cow-barn men, and spent much time currying their horses and cleaning the stalls. Then after breakfast they went forth to the haying or whatever outside job presented itself. They had little traffic with the cows. Jake says this is one reason why they have gone: they and their horses couldn't qualify as cash earners in the eyes of modern cost accounting. The cows were the breadwinners and the horses their servants, and of course servants have been vanishing all over. The number of men on a farm now, Jake says, is determined by the number of cows that must be milked. All hands milk every morning and evening except on the biggest places, which can afford a manager or a utility outside man. Between milkings the men skip off to the fields with their machines. So there is no room for teamsters, and most teams in our country that haven't died off have been sent elsewhere. George Miner says the last one he remembers well was given by Paul Cleaveland to a New Hampshire farmer who was known to be kind. The horses went off in that direction one day looking noncommittally from the back of a truck. Maine, New Hampshire, and Vermont, Jake thinks, are still raising a surplus of able men, but he believes these are being absorbed by war plants. And it might be noted that tobacco-chewing has faded with the other things. The Salisbury Pharmacy sells but a quarter of its old volume, according to Sam Whitbeck, the owner.

In winter, when fields were frozen or covered, the teamsters would spread manure or cut wood or get in the ice. These jobs have mainly disappeared too. My father got his ice from Lakeville Lake, perhaps three miles away, and a month was given to the job each year. The teams and sleighs took a half day for the round trip, and when little we used to bob behind them, tying a Flexible Flier to a back runner. The pace wasn't much, but we could swerve sideways, tip over, and play other tricks, and the snow and cold were bracing—hard snow by the ruts crushed our fingers on the handlebars.

Now the roads are scraped too thin for sleighs, and no ice is harvested anyway. The ice-houses of our neighborhood have become tool-houses, play-houses, or extra spots to put haybales. There is no extra fund of manure to spread in the winter because it is no longer saved and piled up through the summer, and little wood is cut— logs are still burned in fireplaces, but they aren't used much for cooking or basic heating. Farm hands must still cut fence posts, Jake says, and put them up, but there has been a change even in this. Posts are no longer sunk properly by the old lights—planted in specially dug holes—but are sharpened and driven in like stakes; often the sharpening is done with an old buzz-saw, Jake says, rather than an axe; these doings before the war would have been called shiftless and against nature by some farmers. As a boy I read or heard that fences should be "bull strong, horse high, and hog tight." I don't suppose they often were so in fact. The phrase was an ideal, perhaps a slogan I saw in a catalogue. But at least the fences stood up straight. Now labor and wire are so high (most of the nation's barbed wire is in Korea, farmers here think) that little is done to keep fences going. Some stretches sag or lean morosely, some are patched crazily as if by string-saving old ladies. When they get too bad now, Jake says, the farmer just puts electric fencing in and lets the old stuff go. This adds to the air of decay. It should be noted, though, that the decay isn't an overall thing. Our country isn't like sweet Auburn, loveliest village of the plain. All the farms and farmers are still here, though having let hundreds of acres slip back to woods. They are only working differently now, less extensively so far as space goes.

Some farms keep heated workshops in the winter where machines can be overhauled. For the rest they give their men more leisure. Leisure is used differently from in the old days, of course, the year round. Most farm hands' houses have television, it seems, the smaller the house the bigger the antenna. The decline of berry-picking tells something about leisure too. Our mountains grow fine huckleberries, and each August in the old days much of the population turned toward them, devoting all spare time to picking for sale or use. One father and daughter walked up Mount Riga every day of the season, a three-mile climb, and walked down again carrying two twelve- or fourteen-quart pails of berries each. Berries were so cheap that while they lasted my brothers and I each had a soup-plate of them every morning for breakfast, with pilot biscuit broken over them and milk and sugar poured on. Today one can drive a car right up near the berry fields, but they are little disturbed. Most huckleberries on our market, I am told, come from truck gardens in New Jersey; the price is high and we have no more Bourbon breakfasts. For outdoor sports, men of the village lean toward golf and skiing now, which are city men's sports too. They do a good deal of fishing, but in our parts fishing too has taken on more of a weekend, Abercrombie-and-Fitch nature. The lakes and streams are thickly stocked, and trippers from afar mix undistinguishably on them with local men.* There is less hunting with hound-dogs here in the old way, it seems, less gathering of nuts, less of other country pastimes. On the average, as noted above, we have become more like

* See Chapter VII.

white-collar people. There seems to be much gain from this: more freedom from heat and cold and heavy things to lift. What has been lost is part of the touch with nature. Some here call the change progress. Some think it a further fall from Paradise. Some do not judge but take it as it is.

II. THE FAIR

DUTCHESS COUNTY, New York, adjoins Litchfield County, Connecticut, where I grew up, but the two are different. Litchfield is full of rocks, and its landscape seems always stubborn. Dutchess on the other hand—and especially its western side, which drains to the Hudson—has a soft, lush and complaisant air, or so I used to think on my boyhood trips there. We would cross the state line and drive westward, and the stone outcrops of New England would be left behind. The hills would become softer, the grass would turn a deeper green, and a sense of ease and bounty would suffuse the view. It used to affect me as visits to Paris affect some people, and the experience was at its best when we were bound for the Dutchess County Fair at Rhinebeck, a mile or two from the Hudson itself. The Fair was an annual celebration, in August, lasting four or five days, and it far outdid any festivity in our own county.

For a few years when I was in my teens—almost three decades ago—my two brothers and I used to show horses at the Fair, and this would give us a chance to sleep in the stable there for a couple of nights, and join in the carnival atmosphere. During that time we would show and care for our horses, of course, but we would also live on fairgrounds food and enjoy the vivid pleasures of the Midway. We would mix in the crowd, admire the livestock on show, and feast our senses generally. Then, gorged with new impressions, we would come back to our rockbound hills.

These fairs were among the great events of my youth, and they seemed to have deep significance—to symbolize all kinds of truths about our country life. When I grew up I moved away from these parts, losing track of Dutchess County, fairs and all. But this year I had a chance to visit the Fair again, for several days, and I found it as good as ever. It has kept its character too, I learned, though changing a good deal in some respects; and I imagine that in this way, as in others, it is still a good mirror of the countryside.

One change is in size; the Fair is said to be twice as big as in the 'thirties. It runs for a longer time now—six days—and it has spread out a good deal in area. The fairgrounds are on typical farm land at Rhinebeck's northeastern edge—mainly hayfields that are mowed before the opening day. There is a half-mile trotting track amid them, overlooked by an ancient grandstand, and north of this lies a region where the main Fair activities take place; the Midway is there, together with many buildings and tents for exhibits. East of that part, in my boyhood, lay some rolling empty meadows, but this year I found these occupied by a dozen big tents and frame shelters housing livestock, chiefly cattle. In the center of this colony were two smaller judging tents, and I spent a good deal of time in them.

To reach them I would pass through one of the larger shelters where the cattle lived—warm, drowsy places

these were, the sweet smell of dairy cows in them being
mixed with the piney smell of shavings under foot. As a
rule the cattle would be lying down, except for a few
being groomed for showing—one might be having its
horns sandpapered, for instance, while another would be
under the clippers. The clippers would drone away while
electric fans played on the resting animals, and perhaps
a radio would be moaning too with soft music. I would
leave this peaceful spot, reach a judging tent and sit
down in the bleachers there, surrounded by a few dozen
cattle-lovers of all ages. I watched nearly all the breeds
being judged at one time or another, but I concentrated
on dairy cattle rather than beef, and of the dairy breeds
I watched the Ayrshires longest. Ayrshires are lovely
creatures, the cows especially. Their horns curve ahead
and upward, giving a classical look in profile, like that
of cows in India or in old Mesopotamian art. The silhou-
ettes of Ayrshire cows are especially triangular—deep in
the rear from hindquarters to udder, then tapering toward a point through neck and head. They are fine and
delicate. As a rule, too, Ayrshires have much white in
their coloring, spotted by a dark, sunburned brown, almost walnut.

I watched them being shown through a whole afternoon. The judging tent was of yellow-brown canvas,
with its sidewalls rolled up, and a subdued light came
into it, along with wisps of breeze. On the ground lay a
deep bed of sawdust, with a top layer of cream-colored
shavings, and this surface looked almost like foam—
gleaming faintly—in that light. For background noise
there was an incessant mooing of cows and calves in
nearby tents, and against this the Ayrshires paraded
soundlessly on display, their heads held high by their

leadsmen. They moved slowly, with leisure. Their feet sank into the shavings, and as they walked they scuffed these up softly, like spray, leaving straight furrows behind them. The cows were gentle, suggesting deer, and the leadsmen were gentle too—softspoken, kindly men, often dressed in white. They led their cows slowly, perhaps murmuring into their ears, and sometimes they would pinch or prod them to make them stand straight. They seemed especially alert in the bull classes, holding their charges' heads high and tight by the nose-rings, while the latter sauntered along ominously. When the bulls halted, one of them might paw the shavings, throwing them up high above his back. But as a rule nothing moved abruptly in that tent.

The judge was a young, serious man, solidly built, in his shirtsleeves and wearing a maroon polka-dot tie. He seemed well known in the bleachers, and I heard that he had judged Ayrshires last year at the State Fair in Syracuse. He had a microphone at his disposal and engaged in a practice—new to me but universal now in the Fair's livestock classes, I later found—of explaining his judgements in detail. To sit and hear him, while watching the cattle themselves, was almost like attending a course, and I think this was the intent; the Fair had a sense of mission toward educating the farmers to improve their stock. The judge's remarks were detached, if critical, "I would like to see more weight above her rump," he said of one heifer, and of another he complained that she had "too Roman a nose" and was "too coarse in the neck." He spoke cryptically of qualities like "dairyness" and "breed characteristics."

And later in the afternoon, when the older cows came

on, he concentrated more and more on udders, the essential part of dairy cows. He talked of the "veining," "levelness," and "lovely consistency" of various udders on display. Meanwhile the cows paced slowly in the tent, like pallbearers. Their coats were smooth and glossy, and their horns—black at the tips and clam-colored at the bases—shone with a high polish. The afternoon passed. The judging was hurried at the end, to make way for the evening chores—all through the Fair the cows kept to their strict routine of feeding and milking, and their herdsmen had to see them through it, as at home.

Ayrshires actually played a smaller role at the Fair— as they do in Dutchess County as a whole—than some of the breeds I spent less time in watching. Of dairy breeds, the Holsteins seemed most numerous, and are probably most numerous in the county too—they are the big black-and-white cows so common in our landscape. There were Holsteins on every hand, but I have never been much drawn to them as they seem coarse to me, and are presented at these fairs in a rather utilitarian, no-nonsense way—their horns have usually been cut off, for instance, instead of being cherished and manicured. Their color, to me, is relatively cold and uninviting, and so is the color of their milk, which is bluish and low in butterfat. Yet they put it out in great volume, and this makes them well suited for the colossal New York City market, which draws on Dutchess County and favors bulk over richness. Guernseys are important in Dutchess County too, and were important at the Fair, but I have avoided them here for detachment's sake, being prejudiced toward them from childhood association. Jerseys were prominent also—small and dainty with black noses—and they had their devotees. *All* the dairy breeds have their devotees, and feeling runs high among them.

Beef cattle were much in evidence. Mainly they were Aberdeen Angus, black, but there were also many Herefords, red with white faces. Herefords have grown plentiful in Dutchess County only in the last decade or so, but I remember when the Angus were being introduced there in the 'twenties. They were being promoted by a few big landowners and also by the 4H Club, which was encouraging farm children to raise Angus steers for sale as baby beef. The whole venture seems to have prospered since then—partly because of city people who own large country estates and want to keep them in use. Raising beef cattle is a good way to do this, especially in the current labor shortage, as they need much less attention than do dairy cows. Conversely, though, I was told that few real dirt farmers care much for beef cattle, as in that region they yield but a small profit per acre. So to some extent their presence denotes the intrusion of city men into the Dutchess countryside, which is roughly a hundred miles from New York. The dairy cows shown at the Fair represented this same thing in a way too. In the past few decades, I was told, the breeding of such cows has improved immensely there, partly because well-heeled city men have come in and taken up farming as a hobby. They have tried to develop herds with good appearance, rather than scrub collections that would merely give saleable milk. So the quality of all breeds has gone up, and the Fair has benefited.

The Aberdeen Angus shown at Rhinebeck were black, shiny, and prodigiously wide and fat. In principle they were supposed to look rounded, I was told by one expert, instead of angular, which is a quality prized in dairy cows. They had been carefully fed for months to achieve this state, and now they were being dexterously clipped and groomed to accentuate it. Their coats were oiled and curled in waves, or sometimes even combed in chequer patterns. They seemed the very picture of abundance.

Between spells at the cow judging, and at other things, I kept returning to the Midway. I found it gay and pleasant, though a bit cleaned up since the old days. One of the thrills of my youth had been a strip-tease act of so-called Hawaiian dancers that had come to the Fair year after year—it had always been the same show as I remember it, perhaps incorrectly, but with different girls each time. There had been nothing really Hawaiian about these girls except for the name on the canvas out front. They had been blondes or Caucasian brunettes, two or three of them, most often on the thin side, and they had periodically gathered on a platform before their pitch and done a mild shimmy while a man strummed a tune on the banjo, usually *Springtime in the Rockies*. When a handful of men and boys had gathered we would be led inside, where the girls would take off a good deal of clothing for a quarter, and then take off still more for fifty cents if you stayed afterward. The show had not been great art, but it had been instructive, and I have always remembered it as an essential part of fair-going and adolescence. Now it was no more. One of the first things I did on going to the Fair this time was to look for the Hawaiians or their modern counterpart, but I didn't find them. I did find a snappy-looking trailer with some half-dressed girls depicted on its walls and a sign—"THE PALACE OF BAGDAD"—in process of being painted. But this trailer just sat there idly during the six days, and didn't go into action—I assumed it was traveling with some other Midway shows, and might open up at the next stand. As the days wore on I asked a Fair director what the policy was on girl shows, and he said they were forbidden because the public wouldn't stand for them. I assume he spoke the truth, and I suspect the change is related to deep currents in American life, such as the reputed decline in prostitution in our big cities (which in turn may be related to the decline of manual labor everywhere—people being more choosy about what they do). Anyway, the change had occurred, and the Midway was not quite the same.

It was close enough, though. The Fair had two ferris wheels, a merry-go-round, and three or four rides that were more exciting than these. It had a tent with a five-legged dog, a six-legged heifer, and a five-legged sheep. It had a good act by daredevil motorcyclists in a truncated silo. All these were an old story to me, though with a few new twists—the merry-go-round, for instance, had a phonograph in it now instead of a calliope; sometimes it sounded like a jazz orchestra, sometimes like a player piano. A few new things had been added with the changing times, including two sideshows of old Japanese weapons and a good number of "kiddy rides"—little round-abouts with planes, autos, boats, flying saucers, etc., for seats. There was even a roller-coaster for small children, and I felt that this sector of the public had made striking gains, in entertainment possibilities, since I had belonged to it.

The games of chance and skill seemed much as I remembered them, though the former had apparently dwindled in numbers; there was one big bingo palace on the Midway and only half a dozen smaller chance booths, including two or three where you picked up celluloid ducks from a moving stream of water and read numbers on their undersides. Of the skill games I counted ten booths where you threw baseballs at things (such as wooden milk-bottles or rag-doll cats); nine where you threw darts (at balloons or figured boards); and eight where you threw quoits. These seemed quite unchanged from my childhood except for the prizes, the largest of which were big pastel-colored teddy bears now, instead of the kewpie dolls that I remembered. Half a dozen booths had a game that was new to me, in which you tried to land a dime in one of several plates. This was very expensive. You had to pitch the coin from some distance onto the plate, which was flat and shiny, and hope it would stay there, which it almost never did (wet dimes or dimes with chewing gum on them were not allowed). Among the prizes in this game were live parakeets, but I saw none change hands though scores of dimes were thrown away as I watched.

Besides these things there were shooting galleries, skee-ball alleys, and the like. They too were about the same as in the old days—the ducks and clay pipes in the shooting galleries were quite unchanged, for instance— and as I hung round the Midway I came to see in it one of the more conservative strands of our culture. Not even the heightened mechanization, and mobility, of our national life had affected things much. A few of the booths were mounted in trucks and trailers now, but only a few. The rest were in the same old canvas.

The Midway food had changed a bit. The main staples were, as always, hot dogs and hamburgers, but now the latter were made from frozen discs of meat, kept packed together in cylinders and separated by wax paper. To fill an order the cook had only to pull another disc off for grilling, which seemed to reduce the human element somewhat. Freezing had also made it possible to sell fried Jacksonville shrimps at the Fair—sudden death would have been the forecast for anyone found eating shrimps there in the old days. Pizza was another innovation for me too; it was sold as a snack in rectangular portions. I had never heard of pizza when I attended the Fair of old, but now it was part of the American diet, and a fitting one too on occasions like this. Otherwise the provender was much the same, though of course the prices had doubled, more or less. The cooking smells were the same too—onions here, frankfurters there, coffee somewhere else. Then if you left the Midway they yielded to the sweet cow smell or the pungent smell of horses on the trotting track. Even a human, I think, could have learned to find his way by scent about those fairgrounds.

On most days I would get to the Fair early, while the Midway was still buttoned up. The booths would have their canvas fronts lashed shut, and there wouldn't be much life around—a couple of sleepy, seedy men, perhaps, or a woman with her hair in curlers, going for some coffee. These sights would not claim much attention, and you could take in the Midway's natural setting: an asphalt road bordered by the hay-stubble on which the booths were pitched, and then above it all some cool green maple trees. Then if you returned later in the day you would be conscious only of the crowd, the smells, and the sounds—of music, of barkers, and of 22-caliber explosions in the shooting galleries.

I went there on the busiest afternoon of the whole

Fair, a Sunday. There were long queues at the ferris wheels, and I joined one of them, noting that many of the young men were wearing plaid sport shirts. I watched two girls with huge pink puffs of spun sugar, or cotton candy, get into a seat of the ferris wheel, and a few minutes later, when they got off, they had demolished the puffs entirely. Two other girls, in pink dresses, about eleven or twelve years old, tried to squeeze into the line ahead of me, but I frowned and they withdrew. Eventually my turn came, and I stepped up to the seat. I had no partner of my own, but Fate gave me one in the form of a little girl with blonde hair and long black eyelashes, wearing, on a cotton shirt, the green clover emblem of the 4H Club. She was nine years old, she said, and her name was Betty Carol Leary. She came from Staatsburg, a few miles south of Rhinebeck, and her father was in the seat just ahead of us, with a smaller sister and brother. Betty Carol seemed to be a keen member of the 4H Club, which coaches the rural youth in good farming and home-making; she had made several things for exhibit in the 4H building at the Fair, she told me, including a doll-bed, an apron, a pot-holder, some bean-bags, and a watering-can. She had won a blue ribbon with the watering-can and red ribbons with some of the other things, and she said I could go see them if I liked. When the ride was finished I persuaded her to stay on for another. She told me she liked many things at the Fair, but liked the ferris wheel the best, and I could agree with her when we got up there alone in the blue sky, above the green maples, with the Midway's noise a murmur down below.

The ferris wheel was of old, standard design, but fairly new construction—the owner later told me that a wheel like this cost ten thousand dollars now. I think, incidentally, that I know where some of yesteryear's ferris wheels have gone: they are in India, where life is deemed expendable, and I have ridden on a couple in the past few years. They have been run by turbaned, bearded Sikhs, have been patched together with wire, and have creaked and shuddred ominously while turning round. Riding them, and contemplating their unsure joints, I have often thought of Rhinebeck, wondering if I was in the presence of an old friend.

The best show at the Fair—apart, perhaps, from those held nightly at the grandstand—was not in the Midway, but was something extra: the eight-horse hitch of Anheuser-Busch, the Budweiser beer people. These horses, with their wagon and gear, had been brought to the Fair in five big red trailer-vans. While there they were kept in a special tent, which nearly always had a crowd round it. I mingled in this crowd a good deal, and listened to its comments. Many of the people in it didn't know much about horses, but many others did, and the latter seemed to get nostalgic pleasure from what they saw. The Budweiser horses were all purebred draft animals—Clydesdales—of excellent type; and many other fine draft horses—Clydesdales, Percherons, Belgians, and so forth —had been raised in that section in the old days. They had already been dying out in my boyhood, and now they were gone entirely, but it was plain that their memory lingered on. Usually there were some old-timers in the appreciative crowd at the tent, and what they saw was in the best tradition of draft-horse management. There were ten Clydesdales on hand, all of them bay (reddish-brown, that is). They were kept in a row in straight stalls, their magnificent high, square hindquarters being their most prominent feature to the onlooker. From these their thick, strong hind legs led down to wide "feathers" of white hair at their ankles, and then disappeared in deep yellow straw. The horses stood phlegmatically, sometimes stamping their big feet or switching their short docked tails against the flies. They had six grooms, and these would come often to brush them, rub them down and curry them, in time-honored style, making their coats gleam.

The horses were taken out and driven twice a day; and some time before this their driver, a stocky Swiss named Karl Reichmuth, would come and do up their tails. First he would braid and knot the tail itself and then he would tie a red and a white ribbon into it, making a double bowknot and fanning this out into a rosette. Meanwhile lesser grooms, standing on portable benches, would braid red and white ribbons into the black manes above the great arching necks, and to these they would fix red and white imitation flowers, four or five of them. Then the crowd would be moved back and the horses would be led from their stalls, one by one, their big hooves smiting the ground. The grooms would put their massive harnesses on—thick shiny black leather mounted in brass— and would lead them from the tent and hitch them to the high wagon, which was red and white and mounted in brass too.

Finally all the horses would be out and ready, standing two abreast and in four pairs. They were in superb condition: sleek, and with the combination of roundness and squareness that draft-horses have when really fit. Their necks were thick, their shoulders high and straight, and their short backs dipped smartly, rising again to the chunky hindquarters. They would shake their heads and jingle their bit-chains, and would look lovely with all their dressing up. At length Reichmuth would climb up on the box, accompanied by an assistant driver and a chimpanzee, which traveled with the show. He would take the reins in hand—eight of them—and move out, a way cleared for him through the crowd by State troopers. Usually he would go out on the trotting track, the big wagon rumbling. He would jog round to the grandstand and do figure eights before it, the horses' white legs twinkling as they turned. Then he would complete the circuit of the track and go back to his tent. The big horses would tower over the crowd, putting their feet down like sledge-hammers. They would be unhitched and led back to their stalls, to stand again in the deep straw, and if it was a cool evening red-and-green blankets would be put on them.

I talked for a while with Reichmuth, who said he had come to this country when thirteen, and had been working in the Busch family stables when the first display team had been started, after the legalization of beer in the 'thirties. Now there were two teams on the road. Usually they performed on city streets, he said, and they traveled almost like circuses, arriving at a town in their big red trailer caravan and then playing it for a few days. Reichmuth's team had been working on city streets since last December, and all this time he had been keeping them down to a slow walk, because of the slippery pavements. Now, in doing figure eights at the Fair, they had to move quickly—the lead pair often cantered, in fact, while turning—and he said it was hard to train them up again to the new speed. Most of the Budweiser horses had been imported from Scotland, Reichmuth said

—the home of the Clydesdale breed—but a few had been bought in America and Canada. The Busch family was also raising them now—perhaps as a hedge against their extinction elsewhere—and had four stallions and twenty mares at present. Crowds everywhere loved the horses, according to Reichmuth, but he had a bad time keeping children out from under them, as the modern child didn't know that you must avoid a horse's feet, or risk being stepped on. He also told me that his team's harness had cost fifteen thousand dollars in the 'thirties and was practically irreplaceable now. The team seemed like a fine period-piece, all in all, and Reichmuth himself like the master of a nearly lost art—lost but not forgotten, and well suited to this Fair.

I also talked with Fair officials as the days went by. They told me this was the institution's 111th year, and that it had been in bad shape financially in the late 'thirties, but was now out of debt. Attendance and revenue had both gone up steadily for the past ten years. One director explained to me that the Fair was non-profit and "educational," as opposed to certain others, like the well-known fair at Danbury, which are privately owned and run as commercial ventures. New York State and Dutchess County both supported the Fair—they put up the cash prizes for winning exhibits, among other things. This ensured a stress on farm products, though other phases of the local culture might be slighted. During the Fair I talked with an artist, and art patron, who lived in the neighborhood, and he told me that while the Fair had an art exhibit connected with it, this was poor in his opinion. He admitted, however, that the fault should be blamed on people like himself—he said that a good art show could be arranged if a few real artists took an interest in it, and raised some funds and hunted up exhibitors. I also heard that the Fair's flower-show was thought to be less good than in earlier times, though for a different reason: most of the big estates along the Hudson had let their gardeners go since the 'thirties. These matters were side issues, I gathered, where the Fair management was concerned; the management concentrated, understandably enough, on two things—drawing a crowd and drawing good farm exhibits. (There were also many commercial exhibits there—by people selling everything from tractors to chinchillas—but these seemed to need little supervision; they rented their space and thenceforth ran themselves.)

The attendance this year was something like a hundred thousand, counting all six days. I didn't get the last official figures, and anyway I thought they would be misleading. The Fair's admission booths were manned by uniformed Pinkerton men—an innovation this year—and no doubt the latter did as good a job as they could, but I found places where the grounds were entered secretly by children, from nearby fields. Then many who attended the Fair were exhibitors, coming in on passes. It seemed to be very much a family event—two or three generations coming together, in one car, with the children showing some animals—and the line between spectators and participants was a dim one. I gathered that there were many barn-sleepers there too, as in my day. Some were there from solemn duty, being herdsmen and the like. Some were children, there for fun and duty mixed.

The Fair opened on a Friday and ran till Wednesday. This meant, of course, that it played on Sundays too, which was a radical change from the old days, and one introduced only last year. Then there had been several complaints from church groups, an official told me, but this year there had been none. Much the biggest crowds came on Saturday and Sunday, and on both those afternoons I heard the public-address system make several announcements about lost children—or, more strictly, lost parents; the authorities always had the child in hand, and it was the parents that they called for. Some of the children were too young, or too confused, to give their names, and in such cases their appearance would be described. The public-address system was a key part of the Fair, and was used in many ways. "Will the owner of a red Studebaker, licence number so-and-so, please go and move his car," it would say; "it is blocking the entrance to such-and-such an exhibit." Or "Will the Bond Bread man go to such-and-such a booth immediately." At the same time there were dozens of smaller public-address hookups—one at the grandstand, one at the horse-show ring, and innumerable ones in the hands of barkers. They would blare out as you walked around—mechanical-sounding, but less disembodied than one might think. Often you couldn't see the speaker, of course, but you could visualize what he was talking about. All the loud-speakers gave one a better running picture of the Fair.

Among the crowd I heard many voices that spoke with the accents of Queens or the Bronx, and this was a novelty to me; I didn't remember anything like it in my boyhood. Sometimes I even heard an older person with a strong European accent. So far as I could tell, these voices represented a new element of vacationers in Dutchess County, or more likely a permanent influx of clerical and industrial workers who have gone there with a new boom in manufacturing. The biggest single factor in this boom is the International Business Machines Corporation, which has built a new plant near Poughkeepsie and brought many thousands of new residents to the county (one friend of mine, who lives there, now calls the area "Uncle Tom's Cabin" in honor of Thomas J. Watson). Simultaneously with this influx has come the building of some new throughways, and a new bridge across the Hudson, and these things threaten to change the nature of the countryside, toward greater urbanization. That part of Dutchess County was always closely linked to New York City, anyway, as many New York families had big places on the Hudson, President Franklin D. Roosevelt's being the most famous of them. But these families went to the country in search of rural life, by and large, and they intentionally kept their surroundings rustic. Presumably there is no such urge among the new city influx, and one imagines they will make Dutchess County as urban as they can. Yet there was little evidence of this at the Fair now—only some premonitions. It was still very much a farmers' get-together.

The 4H Club kept cropping up in the Fair's activities, and I kept learning more about it. Its emblem must be familiar to many readers: a green four-leaf clover with a white H on each leaf. These H's, I was told by Hayden H. Tozier, Jr., the Dutchess County 4H Club Agent, stand for Head, Heart, Hands, and Health—things the members are urged to put at the community's service. The Club's aim, as defined by Mr. Tozier, is to train boys and girls in agriculture and home-making, to the end of a better farm life in the nation. He said it was America's only government-supported youth organization, and it drew funds from the county, state, and national treasuries. Tozier himself had come to Dutchess County in 1925, straight from Cornell. That year the Club had had 150 exhibits at the Fair, he said, whereas this year it had six thousand. And in 1925 there had been only 150 members in the county, whereas now there were 1350. In the course of this growth the Club had invested in the fair grounds itself and now owned five buildings there— three livestock shelters, a cafeteria, and a dormitory-and- exhibit building. They were worth a hundred thousand dollars, Tozier said, and the money for them had been raised by the boys and girls themselves, through plays, candy sales, and the like. The dormitory-and-exhibit building was the most imposing of the five and was made of concrete blocks. Tozier told me that the two dormitories, upstairs, could sleep a hundred boys and a hundred girls respectively, and that members showing livestock were expected to live in them through the week the Fair lasted. They were also expected to sign up for twenty-one meals in the cafeteria, for which they were charged fifteen dollars.

Whenever I was in the 4H area—it adjoined the general cattle-show area—I saw boys and girls currying, brushing, and hosing down their animals; they were usually beef steers or dairy heifers they had raised from calves. On the Fair's last day, also, I watched some cattle-showing classes for 4H members. Most of the contestants wore white, which is symbolic of hygiene in the milk business, and the boys were apt to have dark snap-on bow ties. Some girls appeared in pedal-pushers and ma- tador pants, which were a new wrinkle to me. The con- testants were judged chiefly for their animals' cleanliness and their own attentiveness. This last was hard on the younger children, for the classes were long, and they would soon be gazing off into space and letting their animals slouch. But the older boys and girls stayed on their toes.

The home-making activities were supervised by Miss Barbara Reed, Mr. Tozier's young assistant. They included demonstrations of household arts besides the exhibit of handicraft goods to which Betty Carol Leary, my ferris-wheel friend, had sent her beanbags, watering-can, and so forth. I looked for these objects, by the way, but could not find them; they were lost in a huge welter of other such things, representing many thousands of girl-hours in work. The demonstrations, which were staged in the afternoons, took about fifteen minutes each and seemed to have been well rehearsed. I stopped one afternoon just as a girl named Martha Merihew had finished showing how to make a fiber-glass lampshade. "Thank you very much for your kind attention," she was saying to a dozen onlookers as she gathered up her things. Next came Barbara Stevensky, who was in her early or middle teens and had brown hair, blue eyes, and a glorious fresh complexion. She wore a crisp white blouse and a white apron over what I think was a dirndl, and with great aplomb she showed how to make blueberry muffins—or rather how to bring them to the baking stage, as there was no oven there. She laid her equipment out, measured her materials with care, sifted some flour, beat up an egg, and mixed things together, explaining the why and wherefore of each step. When she was done a girl named Patricia Lynch began showing how to make French toast. I left then, but came back another time and watched a younger girl, Mary Ann Balis, aged 10, show how to cut up old greeting cards in such a way as to make new ones out of them, for new occasions. Later I looked at the program of all the demonstrations on the bulletin board, and among those I noted were "How to Iron a Man's Shirt," "Feeding the Convalescent Child," "How to Set an Informal Dinner Table," and "How and What to Pack in a Lunch Box."

Also on the bulletin board I saw a notice that bean- and water-shooters were not allowed in the dormitories, and this was not the only hint I got of lighter 4H moments. One morning, in the judging tent, I heard some girls complain of fatigue, because both the cows and the boys had been making too much noise the night before. And another day I heard Miss Reed saying that some of the girls in the dormitory had been pie-ing her bed. She was wondering whether to retaliate by running the girls' pajamas up the flagpole.

I had a special interest in the 4H Club, because in the past few years I have traveled in Asia and have often heard our "Point Four" workers there mention it. These workers have been trying to better the lot of Asia's peasants, who are mainly illiterate and who get little help from their countries' educated youth—the latter usually gravitate to the cities and think rural matters beneath them. So a gap exists between the peasants and all the scientific knowledge that has been developed about their problems, and the Point Four people have sought to bridge this by introducing U.S. farm-extension-service methods, of which 4H-Club work is really a part. I don't know if this will succeed in the end, or even if the 4H Clubs in America do all they are supposed to do. Yet they do seem unique, as a channel for spreading good farm knowledge to the grass roots, and I doubt if any other country comes close to ours now in the literacy and sophistication of its farmers. This side of our culture showed up time and again at the Fair—in the lengthy comments of the cattle judges, for instance, and the flood of reading matter put out by commercial exhibitors there. One got the impression that an effective illiterate farmer is almost an impossibility with us now.

The summer weather on that part of the Hudson is often hot and muggy, but during the Fair this year it was splendid. The first four days were cool and clear, the nights being chilly. Colors were bright in the sunlight, and the fairgrounds were beautiful when you noticed them behind the hurly-burly: green meadow-grass with green elms and maples, under a pure blue sky (the elms a bit browner and dingier than the maples, perhaps from the blight). The drawback, inevitably, was dustiness. As the days passed I noticed that the dust was coming through my clothes more and more, making for a grimy feeling. On Monday, by the horseshow ring, I heard a woman complaining. "I just washed my hands," she told a friend, "and the mud practically ran off me." Yet it was pleasant withal, the scene sparkled so. Then on Monday night and Tuesday we had showers, which laid the dust somewhat. On Tuesday morning puddles glistened in the sun along the empty Midway.

I wandered here and there through the Fair. There were all kinds of small, miscellaneous operations going on—booths advertising shoes, kitchen appliances, hearing aids, hi-fi equipment; booths putting out literature on Christian Science, cancer, cerebral palsy, birth control. There was a small post-office on the grounds and also an itinerant artist, who engraved profiles with a stylus on what looked like copper leaf; these seemed good too, and they cost only one or two dollars, depending on the size; the artist, a burly, fair-haired young man, had a tape-machine that sometimes played Offenbach can-can music, as if to conjure up thoughts of Toulouse-Lautrec. There were many rich-looking displays of hay, grain, and ensilage; vegetables and fruits; and canned goods, cakes, and pies—shown mainly, I think, by Grange organizations.

Dutchess County is a good apple region, and has been that all through my lifetime—far better than the neighboring parts of Connecticut—so inevitably there was an apple-promoting booth at the Fair. It gave out leaflets and sold Early McIntoshes, drinks of ice-cold cider, and bottles of an apple syrup, recommended for pancakes and the like (I tried some of this and found it good, but with the apple flavor rather weak). I visited the apple booth often, to pick up a McIntosh or a cup of cider, and from talks with the people there I gathered that apple-raising in the county had declined somewhat—with fewer trees now, and fewer orchards too. The average size of orchards was becoming larger, though, as the need for costly spray equipment was increasing; Dutchess trees got sprayed about twenty times a year now, I gathered.

By the way of more immediate news, I learned that the apple crop this year was bad, because of killing frosts in the spring. These had taken 35 per cent of the crop in some places, though not beside the Hudson; there the situation had been saved either by the nearness of the water, with its warmth, or by the slope of the land, which made the cold air run off instead of lingering in pockets (the apple-booth people disagreed between these reasons).

There were many signs at the Fair of further mechanization in the countryside. The latest big development in this, to judge by what I saw, has been the so-called three-point hitch, which enables tractors to act as derricks now, lifting weights, by hydraulic systems, instead of merely pulling things as they used to. Many applications of this principle were on show in the farm-machinery exhibits—tractors with scoop shovels, with fork lifts, with ditchers, with manure lifters, and with post-hole diggers. I even heard one tractor salesman tell of a grave-digging attachment his company made; it would dig a grave with nice straight sides in only a few minutes, he maintained. I learned, too, that diesel power is making big inroads in the tractor world, and that Ford tractors from the British Isles are being sold here more cheaply, even allowing for the duty, than they could be if locally made.

The tendency to put more and more things on wheels was also evident at the Fair (though not especially, as I have said, in the Midway). Near one of the cattle-shelters I saw an impressive operating-table at work. Its surface—rather like a slatted gate—would be vertical while a cow was led up beside it and tied to it, by various slings; then a power attachment would tilt it over to a horizontal position, and the cow would suddenly be lying flat. This gadget was mounted on wheels and hitched behind an auto. There were also comprehensive displays at the Fair of "mobile homes"—trailers, in ordinary parlance—and several little foreign cars and foreign motorcycles. Day by day in every way, it seemed plain, the farmer rolls faster and faster.

The Fair had enough variety of living things on show, I would guess, to rank with the better menageries. The Northern Dutchess Rod and Gun Club had a display there that *was* a menagerie, in fact, containing a bobcat;

a pond of beavers, geese, and ducks; a case of snakes; a covey of bobwhite quail; many other animals of the region; and even an armadillo and a kangaroo. In the live-stock shelters there were swine, and sheep, and fancy poultry—strange, decorative birds with topknots, lacy feather-patterns and so forth. On the last two days in the horse-show ring, there were also pulling contests between yokes of oxen—tall, strong, quiet animals that seemed to have come from the more primitive parts of New England. A big crowd watched them take turns at hauling weights along the ground, with considerable effort, on a stoneboat (which would then, ironically, be hauled right back into place by a tractor).

The horse-show itself had changed since my youth. Then it had been a two-day affair, as I recall it, dominated by hunters and Kentucky saddle-horses, which had all been ridden in the Eastern style, with English saddles. Now these categories had been cut down to one day of showing, but the show as a whole had been expanded to three, with a day each devoted to children's ponies and to Western-style horseflesh. The Western-style day was thoroughly filled up with its various classes, and some of these were really big, with more than twenty entries. Several of the horses shown seemed of good type too, recalling the smarter-looking cowponies in Will James drawings. Most of the exhibitors were children, and nearly all of them wore sombreros with the brims rolled up on either side. They had the standard accoutrements of Western saddles and Navajo saddle-rugs, and a few of them even wore fringed leather jackets. In the ring they jogged past like the Lone Ranger, amid plumes of dust.

This great emphasis on cowboy stuff was new to me, and I wondered how it had come about. Dutchess County has two packs of foxhounds, and in my day its equestrian life had been dominated by people following British patterns almost exclusively. I felt that the new movement could not have been recruited from the children of these Eastern-style families, as tradition is strong in such matters, and I confirmed this by inquiries. As far as I could learn, rather, the new cowboys came from two other sources: from newly prosperous farming families and from the influx of metropolitan wage-workers—it was in the crowd round the Western-style horseshow that I heard city accents most consistently. The inspiration of the Western style had come from the movies, television, the radio, and the comics, acting mainly on the children. But I learned of some practical reasons too. For one thing horses and equipment kept in the Western style do not need the ceaseless grooming required by the Eastern, with its high standards of smartness, and hence are more suited to a time of labor shortage. For another the Western style permits of brighter colors in clothing, and this appeals to many women (or so I was told by the woman manager of a saddlery booth at the Fair). For all these reasons the Western-style heresy was flourishing, causing a few eyebrows to be raised among old-school Dutchess horsemen—"It is like High Church and Low Church," a detached friend of mine remarked about the conflict. The new fashion had little importance in itself, I felt, as the type of riding one does is so academic and subjective a question now. Yet the change did seem to stand for a revolution of sorts—for wealth being shared by unaccustomed hands.

Each night there was a big public entertainment before the grandstand, and I went to a couple of them. An official told me the Fair always had a problem in choos-

ing these shows, which had to be popular and to draw
well—they had to make a hit on the first night or two
especially, so word of mouth would get round. The best
attraction in the Fair's history had been an ice show, a
few years ago, but the present policy was to use general
TV entertainments, and this seemed to be working well.
The first show I saw was an assemblage of rock-&-roll
performers—a trio of instruments, a quintet of the same,
and two or three singers. The trio came first, and its
music seemed mainly to be built on things like *The St.
Louis Blues* and *The Darktown Strutters' Ball*, much
elaborated. The players were out on a bright-lit platform
in the infield, with the track curving round past them
into the dark. In the open grandstand, chilly with the
cool night, I was surrounded by a crowd mainly of young
people, and mainly of girls at that—bobby soxers, I suppose they were (or perhaps bobby-stockingers, for many
of them wore shorts and knee-length hose). While the
trio played the young people began shaking the benches
—sitting there snapping their fingers, and doing something like the charleston with their feet. The music
warmed up and they began playing hand games with
each other, rather like pat-a-cake, pat-a-cake, baker's
man. At that stage I left for some time, to check on the
Midway. When I came back the quintet—four strings
and a set of drums—was on the stage, and the party had
warmed up further. It was a cozy atmosphere, with musicians and audience both rocking. But that phase didn't
last long either. It was near the end of the program now,
and before long girls in small packs began running down
to the track and standing before the stage. More and
more of them ran, and boys too, encouraged by the players. They hurried through the shadows as if in a pagan

ritual. At length I followed, more slowly. The track before the stage was covered with young people now, and the quintet and trio were brought on together—eight instruments. The musicians played with more and more abandon, stamping and stamping and shaking their moppy heads, while the young folks jittered on the track in the floodlights. Then the show ended, and the players were mobbed for autographs. They withdrew to their dressing-tent after a while, but the children followed them there, and the show people got cold feet and called the State troopers. A couple of the latter were standing by when I left, but really the crowd was well behaved.

The other entertainment I saw was a variety show called *The Midwestern Hayride*. It had elements in it of hill-billy music, of rock & roll, of square-dancing, and of jitterbugging, along with jokes. "Rhinebeck's a nice little town," the star girl singer declared at one point. "I like the way it's laid out. . . . Yes, I do. . . . I don't know how long it's been dead, but I sure like the way it's laid out." Such humor was scattered in between songs, dances, yodeling, and clowning, and there was an imitation of Elvis Presley that went over well. Again there was warm enthusiasm in the audience, and a really jolly atmosphere. There were a number of older people on hand this time, and I gathered that many of them were acquainted with the show from television. I had never gone to the grandstand entertainments in the old days, thinking them too expensive and probably too dull. I regretted this now, wishing I could compare the old with the new. I suspect there is a stronger continuity between them than is generally admitted, by either the press agents or the denouncers of things like rock & roll. But I can do no more than speculate on this.

There is one change in the mass-entertainment line that I *can* report, though—namely the disappearance, without a trace, of a brass band that used to come annually to the Fair, where it would play Sousa marches and the like. I had been much stirred by this music, whose throbbing rhythm had permeated the fair-grounds, and I missed it now.

A mere dark cave by night, the grandstand turned by day into a piece of architecture. It was long and barnlike, big enough to hold a thousand. It must have been a fine gingerbread structure once, and it still had traces of nice jigsaw work. But through the decades these had been overwhelmed, and almost patched out, by later and rougher carpentry. The original color, or at least an early one, had been brown, but not much of this was left —nor, indeed, was much left of even later coats, including near-white and battleship gray. Stretches of these colors could be made out, the paint peeling or sunk to a neutral dimness, but the tone that really dominated was the gray of weathered wood. The thin columns at the grandstand's front were old too, and scarred with nail-holes. Yet it was a distinguished place, airy and comfortable, looking out on the track, and beyond it to the rustic landscape.

In the infield just before the stand a small asphalt oval had been built, since my day, and on Saturday afternoon some midget-auto races were held there. About a score of cars took part, some of them painted in red, yellow, pink, green, and other bright colors. They sparkled like toys in the sunlight, on the dark track with the green grass beside it. When racing they swirled and roared about the oval, with almost hypnotic effect. The sight was thrilling too, and the better drivers habitually came out of the turns with their left—inner—front wheels off the ground. Yet the races were probably less dangerous—so small were the cars—than they seemed. In one of them, indeed, five cars got in a smash-up all together, yet no driver was hurt badly.

The harness races, for pacers and trotters, were held on Monday and Tuesday afternoons, and in the days before I would stop from time to time at the stables, which were near the turn to the backstretch. Horses would be arriving. A boy might be cleaning harness by one stall, and a blacksmith tacking on a shoe by another. There would be horse-smells there, and smells of hay and saddle-soap. A few horses would be working on the track, some of them going fast and raising a lather. Their hoofs would beat smartly on the packed earth as they whizzed by, their drivers crouched forward on the little sulkies. I remembered scenes like it in my youth, and I found a nostalgia at the track like that round the Budweiser horses. Before the races began a Fair official told me that the crowds they drew were enthusiastic, but had been dwindling year by year through old age. Then on the morning of the first races I met four men from my own township—Salisbury—in Litchfield County, who had brought a pacer over. The horse was owned, and was to be driven, by a young doctor, Bob Noble, but two of the men with him were older farmers, Paul Cleaveland and George Miner, who had taken to harness-racing a little while ago, I suspect because they missed horses while riding about on their tractors. Paul Cleaveland told me how they had restored an old trotting-track in Salisbury township, near his farm. It had been built in the eighteen-nineties, he said, and had been used for about ten years. Then hay had been cut off it for another decade or two, after which it had been let go entirely. It had grown up in brush and second growth, with elms and other trees twenty feet high, and in restoring it a bulldozer had worked for twelve days. Paul Cleaveland remembered going to races there as a boy, near the turn of the Century, and he said most of the towns and villages roundabout had had tracks then, with the men of the neighborhood bringing their driving-horses to them.* In regions like North Vermont and far upstate New York the tracks had never been abandoned, he thought, but in these parts they had, though some were now being revived again. At the Salisbury track there were half a dozen horses now, George Miner told me, and they raced informally every Sunday.

The crowd in the stand that afternoon was smaller than that at the midget races, and older without doubt— all kinds of country-looking old men, often smoking cigars. Sometimes acquaintances would meet who hadn't seen each other for years, and they would have a big reunion, discussing old times happily. There were three races, each of two heats, making six in all. Trotters or pacers have to get a running start when they race, with the position of each horse assigned in advance, and in the old days this had caused many delays, one horse or another getting out of line so the whole lot would have to be called back. Now, though, they were started with a moving barrier mounted on a Cadillac touring-car. After parading to the post they would gather behind the car in the backstretch, each in its allotted place, and would sweep down on the starting-line all in order. Then the

* The Salisbury track had been related to the presence of iron-industry money in the town. See Chapters V and VI.

car would pull ahead and out of their way. Despite this
improvement it was like old times to see the horses
thundering past the grandstand, the drivers leaning forward in their bright colors, whip in hand. The old men
in the stand would pick favorites in the race and would
say "Watch that number-one horse," or "Watch that
number six," or "Watch that little sorrel." Their picking
was not expert—it was done not by knowledge but by
fancy, when the horses came on the track. The pickers
just enjoyed the races, it seemed, and they enjoyed them
more if they had a horse to whom they gave passing alle-
giance. There was no betting at these races either, and
the spirit was different from the one I hear prevails on
the big new trotting tracks near the city. It was mainly
love of horses, and memories of them, that brought the
crowd out here. And the horses did look lovely too, with
their long manes and tails, and their gaunt bellies and
deep chests, as they trotted past, extended.

Doctor Noble's pacer, named Murph, was a reddish
chestnut, and he looked well with the Noble colors: blue
and black. He didn't race too brilliantly. He finished fifth
in one of his heats and third in the other—about the
middle of the lot—and later on George Miner told me
that the pace here was faster than what they were used
to on the home track. This was after Murph had been
washed, scraped, and rubbed down following the second
heat, by his crew of handlers. They had put a blanket on
him, and George was walking him round to cool him out.
He seemed content enough as he discussed the race, and
I don't think any of Murph's handlers was disappointed.
They took him home in a trailer that night, and the next
day they brought another pacer, named Zip-up, dark
brown and aged fourteen. That second day the sky was

black, and it rained during some of the races. This didn't seem to matter much; the track could use the moisture, and several of the drivers put on short plastic raincoats, a modern wrinkle, through which their colors showed plainly. Doctor Noble and George Miner had each worked Zip-up hard in the morning, after their arrival, but even so he was nervous, that being his temperament, and he had to be led round incessantly before he raced.

He did about as well as Murph had, finishing near the middle of his two heats. But again I don't think this was looked on as failure by his handlers. I think they had a successful time just through coming there and taking part. And that seemed true of virtually all the fair-goers. Each got what he sought and went home satisfied.

III. THE FAUNA

NINE YEARS AGO I looked into certain changes that had taken place, since my boyhood, around my home town here.* I found that humans in our countryside had withdrawn somewhat from nature, and that the life and landscape had changed accordingly: many once open fields had gone back to brush, and many former woodsmen, or their sons, had grown domesticated. Since making that inquiry I have often come back to Salisbury, and I have spent two complete autumns here, in '59 and '61. I have walked in the woods and talked with the neighbors, and I am ready now to make a new report, the burden being, this time, that our animal world has changed a good deal too—often because of the human changes, though sometimes not.

The main faunal change, to my eye, has been a great increase in certain animals and birds—a rushing in of nature, as I see it, to the vacuum man has left. We have more of deer, of beaver, of raccoons, of ruffed grouse, and of wood-ducks—to name a few of the more obvious —than we had in the 'twenties and 'thirties, when I was young. We have more of certain fish, too, and of certain small birds, though I am less well qualified as an ob-

* See Chapter I.

server of these last. To me as a boy they seemed less dramatic than the larger creatures—those that were hunted, hooked, or trapped—and I paid less attention to them.

Along with the increases there have been some related, or probably related, decreases. There have been other decreases that are simply mysterious, so far as I know. And then some totally new animals—possums, for instance, and porcupines—have come into our land by migration. The changes are complex and poorly understood, yet they have brightened our lives a lot and are worth recording.

The human change most influential on the wild-life, almost certainly, is the growth of the conservation idea. This is a philosophical change, away from the frontier spirit, that has affected nearly everyone here—even our most carefree poacher, now, could give a well-informed lecture on conservation theories. The change is expressed most effectively, of course, in protective game laws, and these seem wholly responsible for the comeback of some species—of, say, the wood-ducks. When I was a boy wood-ducks were nearly extinct here—I never saw one in that whole period. But last September and October I often saw a flock of them—more than a dozen—on the Miners' brook, which is two miles from my brother Jake's house, where I have been living. The birds were small and dainty by duck standards. The females were brown, but the drakes were brightly colored, with red and white on their faces and with long greenish head-plumes. That brightness would show up on a sunny afternoon, as they swam on the narrow stream, and I would catch glimpses of it as I walked up. I never got too close to the ducks— they would fly away quickly, and softly, over the fields—but it was exciting to see them at all. And then

Mrs. Lincoln Foster, who lives in the next township, has told me that she hand-raised a little wood-duck last summer—it had been hatched in a tree by her house and then got separated from its mother. All in all, wood-ducks are very prevalent now, and tame.

They have been brought back by a wholly closed season—no shooting of them at all—over the past few decades. In the 'thirties I did some fly-fishing, and I remember that certain flies, which were supposed to use wood-duck feathers in their wings or tails, were being made with feathers instead from Chinese mandarin ducks—that was the story put out, anyway, for the law was strictly enforced. And the same spirit—of strict conservation, though with reasonable open seasons—has increased nearly all the well-known ducks and geese—the migratory waterfowl—in North America since the 'thirties. I have seen scores of geese at a time—and have heard them honking—over my brother's house in the fall, and that, for me, is something new. The fortunes of these migrants, in general, are not local to Salisbury, and I shan't go into them. But wood-ducks *are* local, for they nest here and stay through the summer. Mallards do the same, and there are more of them, too, than in my boyhood. Several times in the past fall I have scared up one, two, or three of them, from a stream, while walking. They would be bigger than the wood-ducks, though rather like them in coloring. They would jump nearly straight up from the water—sometimes quacking—and would continue to gain altitude.

Our abundance of deer owes a lot to conservation too, but it owes as much, perhaps, to the changes in our farming life. We had many deer in my boyhood, but we have more now, and I think they are tamer. Last autumn at least four of them frequented the swamp behind my brother's house. I would see them while walking through there, on the nearly abandoned tracks of the Central New England Railroad—I would see their white tails bounding off in the twilight (and time and again I would see their hoofprints between the ties). Then toward December they began coming near the house itself—invading an old apple orchard that my bathroom window looked on. I would see two or three of them coming in the winter-morning darkness—they would step along, twitching their tails rhythmically, nuzzling the ground for apples, and pausing often to look and listen. On the orchard's far side—against a red-brown winter hedgerow there—they would be nearly invisible. But then they would come closer—to within twenty or thirty yards—and would contrast beautifully with the black trees and the still-green grass.

Later I saw a deer feeding in the orchard at noon, even, on a bright day with patches of snow around. It grazed quietly, but raised its head in my direction when the house made a noise—when the wind scraped a lilac-branch, for instance, against the clapboards. The deer would look at the house awhile, with its white-lined ears —all edged in black—cocked forward. Then it would lower its head and return to the apple-hunt or whatever it was engaged in—twitching its tail and seeming undisturbed. It was a joy to watch, of course, and I did nothing else for several minutes. Then a car came in our drive, and the deer trotted off.

One may shoot deer in Connecticut with a bow and arrow, within limits, or with a gun if one has written permission from the landowners. These rules keep out the more ferocious weekenders, but they needn't stop a local man, and anyway the deer laws are taken less seriously, one suspects, than strict enforcement requires. Our deer are so plentiful, and do so much damage to crops and gardens, that the sentiment for their protection is not unanimous. Some experts say that the wartime meat shortage helped break it down too, and then the coming of the deep-freeze has had an effect. Large stores of venison can be kept in a freezer—ending the old need for quick consumption—and such venison can masquerade as beef if anyone gets nosey. There seems scant reason, on the whole, why a local woodsman can't almost live off venison, and perhaps some do. But the woodsmen themselves have been dwindling in number—which has helped the deer negatively—and meanwhile our changing landscape has helped them positively.

Deer like to browse on saplings, and they like peace in their environment, and they have been getting more of both in Salisbury, thanks to our postwar farm revolution. The Federal Government has hastened the trend, moreover, by paying farmers not to plant grain. Often the farmers plant Christmas trees instead. The deer don't like the Christmas trees themselves much, but they like the wild growth in between them. Then our landowners have been changing in type, along with our landscape. We have fewer dirt farmers all the time, and more of what amount to year-round summer people—rich outsiders who have been drawn here by our good schools, low taxes, and beautiful scenery. The newcomers often buy dairy farms. They may keep these running—or engage dirt farmers to do so—but they may also take them out of production or convert them to beef-raising, which is a less intensive use—another backward step toward thickets. Meanwhile the newcomers are usually more conservation-minded than the old dirt farmers—less apt to see deer as food-sources, primarily, or plant-destroying vermin—and they often stop deer-hunting on their land entirely.

The newcomers may well be crack shots—frequenters of Scotch moors and Southern duck-blinds; but they are not woodsmen in the way our old farmers have been. The day's work often took the old farmers into the woods, where deer knowledge is to be had, but it seldom takes the newcomers there.

Knowledge of ruffed grouse—colloquially known here as partridge—is likewise to be gained from working in the woods; and these birds, which share honors with the deer as our great forest spectacle, have been teeming here for a decade or two. In the 'twenties and 'thirties, as I remember it, there were years when one hardly ever saw a grouse. It was believed then that they went in cycles—that they would be plentiful for a while; that their food supply would then wane, as a result, and their enemies wax; that the partridge would die off; that the food would therefore come back and the enemies diminish; and that the birds would once more swell to plenty. It was sometimes said that the cycle took seven years, and that the main natural enemy in it was a parasite lodging on the grouse's body. If the theory was true, something must have thrown the cycle off, because it seems pretty certain that our grouse have been roughly constant, in their high abundance, throughout the 'fifties at least. Experienced hunters have told me this, and I have got the same impression from being here, and walking in the woods, in '59, '61, and also the winter of

'52-'53. In each of those periods I have flushed about the same number of birds (per afternoon of walking), and more than in any but the best years of my youth.

Grouse are thrilling things to put up—they are brown birds, the size of chickens; they often lie quiet for a long time; and then they rise from near your feet with a great roaring of their wings. They fly quickly and crookedly, often getting trees between themselves and you. They are sometimes found in barberry thickets, abandoned apple orchards, etc., where they like to feed, and these may border on open farmland. But more usually, perhaps, they will be deep back in the woods, sheltering in brush or hemlock trees. I have put scores of them up in the past fall, sometimes not seeing them at all—only hearing them—but often getting a good look at them. Once I even followed a pair of grouse that were walking calmly, the male with his ruffles extended, on the edge of an asphalt road near the village. I followed them for several yards, till they took flight, and that was another new experience.

The cycle theory is too deep and mysterious—too technical—for me to comment usefully on, but I feel sure there is at least one other pattern of change in the grouse population. I believe they make a lasting, non-cyclical adjustment to a long-term change in their food supply and the enemy pressure on them. I have read that when the Pilgrim Fathers reached New England, the grouse were so plentiful, and so unwary, that they could be knocked off hemlock limbs with clubs.* Those fat times are long gone from Salisbury, but so, I suspect, are the lean times of my childhood. It so happens that the pres-

* My authority for this statement, which some readers have questioned, is an article by Tom Dolan in *Sports Afield*.

sure from another partridge enemy, the fox, has been off
of late—our foxes were nearly wiped out, a decade ago,
by mange—yet I believe that slackened human pressure
figures too. I suspect that all this good news has helped
the grouse to weaken the cycle—such as it may have
been—or even to throw it off entirely.

Grouse—or partridge—hunting is not easy here. A dog
can be of some help in it, but not much help—the hunter
himself must beat the woods carefully. In Salisbury this
is apt to mean scratching through hemlocks and clam-
bering up and down black-rock ledges—all while carrying a gun—and then being frustrated by the birds' sudden takeoffs and twisty flight. Such hunting demands
patience and ardor, and one can't be surprised if the
newcomers (with certain notable exceptions) prefer to
lay off the partridge and hunt straight-flying pheasants,
with a dog, in open fields.

The diversions in our countryside—cars, radios, bowl-
ing, skiing, etc.—are more widespread than in my boyhood, and this has inclined our native sons, as well, to
be easier on the wildlife. One factor in the upsurge of
raccoons here—though a less important one, perhaps,
than certain changes in the fur-trade—has been a big
decrease in nocturnal coon-hunting with dogs. When I
was a boy several men in Salisbury had coon-dogs—so
many that my brothers and I could nearly always per-
suade one of them to take us out, on short notice, of an
evening. There are still two or three of that sort here, but
the rest of our manhood stays home to watch TV, and
partly because of this our coon population is exploding. I
saw more dead coons by the road last fall, I believe, than
I had seen in my whole life before that, and I heard a

lot about their depredations, especially among the town's sweet corn (it seems they like corn of every kind, but especially the "sweet" corn that is grown for humans rather than animals). I heard of one farmer near here who sought to protect a patch of field corn—the animal kind—that he was growing by planting eight rows of sweet corn all around it. The scheme worked well, I was told; the coons laid all the sweet corn flat—by pulling the stalks down to take the ears off—but left the other almost untouched. Salisbury's gardeners, though, who have been trying to grow sweet corn alone, have had a worse problem. Their best solution, they say, has been to use electric fencing—perhaps borrowing it from a dairy-farmer, or erstwhile dairy-farmer, who got it originally to keep his cows in pasture. Corn surrounded by a double electric fence, about eight inches off the ground, is said to be fairly safe from the raccoon hordes.*

The coons also climb into apple trees and take bites from the apples, though this isn't too important here, for we no longer raise good apples anyway. They cause more headaches, perhaps, by raiding the cabins on Mount Riga, our town's main eminence, when the owners are away. They get into the kitchens, according to Spalding McCabe, whose family has a few cabins on the mountain, and once inside they open the cupboards, which they can do quite easily with their hand-like paws. They like cocoa, flour, and sugar, Spalding says, and they scatter these lovely powders around a kitchen, perhaps adding a few syrups to the mess. Coons are rated very clean animals personally, but that doesn't extend, it seems, to their housekeeping in strange premises.

* A man in Dutchess County solved the problem by painting his cornstalks with creosote.

The fur-trade changes behind the coon explosion include, of course, the near-disappearance of the coonskin coat, but there is also a general slump in fur prices and a general drift away from trapping by our men and boys. In the 'twenties a great many boys here would have a few traps out, or even extensive trap-lines; they would catch fur-bearing animals often or not often, according to their skill; and they would take the pelts to a dealer in Canaan—five miles away—or would send them to one of several big companies that put out catalogues to promote the trade (the Herskovits Fur Company of Chicago was the one best known to my brothers and myself; its catalogue listed all kinds of furs and quoted tempting prices on them according to size, color, condition, etc.). Trapping could be lucrative, in those days, for a really woodsy boy or man; and while it had its cruel side, it did get even the most inept of us out of doors and taught us a little more about nature. Now our boys are keen on other things. A few of them still trap, and so do a few old-timers here, but it's no longer a big feature of the life.

The price-slump in furs surprised me, by its sharpness, when I looked into it last fall. My chief informant was Clayt Morey, a leading member of one of our trappingest families—he has just left the trap-lines himself, in middle age, but has broken a son in to them. "Coons pay nothing now," he told me when I saw him. "So there are lots of them around. Twenty-one years ago a good coon would pay ten to eighteen dollars. Now you have to have a damn good one to get even two. It's the same with mink. I've got as high as forty dollars for a mink, and now you're lucky if you get eight. So there are lots of *them* here too." And there are lots of muskrats, he added, though he called them mushrats, which is their universal name in Salisbury. "The mushrats were getting thinned out good a while ago," Clayt said, "but now they're back again. You can get only a dollar and a quarter now, you know, for a good rat in prime condition, though I used to average three dollars and fifteen cents for them—throughout the season, in both good and bad condition."

Clayt talked on about these changes and what they had led to—to fewer rabbits here, for instance, because of increased mink and weasels. He also touched on the causes of the price-slump, including the popularity of ranch-bred furs. He didn't mention synthetic fur substitutes, but I feel sure that these too are important, and that they, along with the fur-farming, are a close part of the trend I have been describing—the movement away from nature toward the artificial. The older human community here was well joined with the animal world—it preyed on that world, observed it cannily, and passed time endlessly in seeking out its haunts. Those older humans were, in fact, more animal than we in Salisbury are today. We current humans are more abstract and mechanical. With our new technology we exploit the wild things less. And we understand them less—pay less attention to them—though luckily they seem to thrive on that.

I am not stealthy enough myself to get many glimpses of the now-prevalent fur-bearers, but last fall I did have a few striking experiences in that line. I got four close looks, for instance, at muskrats, and each was better than any in my youth. Two of the rats I saw in a beaver pond, beside the C.N.E. tracks, and the other two in the Miners' brook. One of the latter I first saw on the brook's surface, as I was walking along. It dived, but came up again be-

neath the roots of an old stump in the opposite bank—I
could see its gray snout above the shadowy water there.
The rat was quiet, moving just a little, and I stood and
waited. Then it came out and sat, in the open, on a root
just below the water's surface. Then it swam a short distance. Then it suddenly churned back noisily, as if in
alarm; but it took up its seat again, quite calmly, on the
root. Then it swam downstream and around and about,
sometimes hiding under a bank, sometimes moving un-
concernedly out in the current. It was like a big wet
house rat, but fatter—blunter—and with fluffier fur.

The other rat I saw in that brook came running down
the bank, from a cow-pasture, with vegetation in its
mouth. It splashed in under the bank, then later moved
into midstream and hung there awhile, treading water—
wheeling and standing, in the current, like an East River
tug. It seemed very bold, as had the first rat—and as did
the two, also, on the beaver pond—and I cannot doubt
that muskrats are legion among us now—are having a
real renaissance. And then when walking near streams
last fall I often heard loud plops—far louder than the
frogs make. I had occasionally heard such things in my
youth, but to hear them so very often was a new experience. It surely means more muskrat, I believe, and perhaps more otter too.

This brings me to the crowning act, so far, in my Salisbury circus, which I shall record here at the risk of being
set down as the local Munchausen. Last October I followed an otter at close range—almost accompanied it—
along the Miners' brook for half an hour. This event was
beyond my wildest dreams, yet I jotted down notes while
it was happening, and I hereby present their substance. I
had just crossed an asphalt road, entered a pasture of the

Miners', and started down their stretch of the brook, when I heard a splash behind me. I stopped and looked around, but saw nothing for a moment. Then the otter— which had presumably left the water again, since the splash—came up toward me on the bank. It was like a grayish weasel, but much bigger—a couple of feet long —and its fur had the same wet-ratty quality as I have noted in the muskrats. A slanting log lay along the bank, fifteen or twenty feet away from me, and the otter went to and fro on this, moving in the silent inexorable way that belongs to the weasel family. I thought it might be hunting frogs, but a frog jumped in as I was thinking so, and the otter paid no attention. I thought also it might be incapacitated—not quite itself—for it had a wound on its back—a skinned patch the size of a postage-stamp—as if it had been in a fight. Yet it moved very deftly. In time it did re-enter the stream, and it swam across and up it in a beautiful way, like a torpedo. It swam almost to the bridge, beneath the road, and then got out on the other bank. Once there, it moseyed along downstream as if hunting. Sometimes it was hidden in the brush over there, and sometimes it emerged—weaving between the bushes, up and down and round about, with an almost serpent motion. It seemed less serpentine, though, on one occasion, when it came into plain view—traveling along a sandbar—for many minutes. It still went slowly and kept sniffing, but it seemed less mysterious—seemed more the straight-man on that flat, exposed terrain. It seemed almost like a low-slung dog.

Farther down the otter came to some obstacles—trees, for instance, growing right up from the brook—and it swam around these, swirling casually in the water, and emerging on their downstream sides. Its shifting, from element to element, was hardly perceptible.

After a while togetherness with the otter grew so commonplace—its thrill so dulled by familiarity—that I began looking for other sights and lost track, for quite some time, of the otter itself. But our best encounter was yet to come. I drifted down along the bank for many yards—and many minutes—and was standing, vaguely, by a dead elm tree when the otter came right up toward me, passing the elm, till it was hardly two feet distant. It kept on coming, as if it might even climb my legs, and I was so startled that I made a false move. It scuttled off down the bank then, but a minute later it came back on the tree's other side. Again it came within about two feet, and it stood there while we gazed at each other. It had a pink nose, whiskers, dark eyes, and brownish-grayish fur except for the bare patch. It looked at me awhile, then turned and vanished down the bank again. It entered the stream and swam away, making big splashes—I thought playfully—as it did so.

I used to read about things like that in the nature books, but I never hoped to witness them. Now the books have been coming true for me, and I give thanks to man's new ways—I don't see how, in my boyhood, an otter could have afforded such nonsense—a trap, or bullet, or other calamity would have ended it. Starvation might have ended it, in fact, but even that threat has been weakened along the Miners' brook, for the water there is throbbing, nowadays, with trout put in by Albert Tilt, a newcomer who owns the second farm downstream. Mr. Tilt is like our other newcomers in being no farmer—and in having more than a farmer's income to spend on his place—but he is fairly special, too, in being close to the wildlife. He knows where the partridge are, for instance, and hunts them hard, and he is a keen fisherman who stocks his stream with thought.

His stocking system is complex, but essentially he plants three kinds of trout—brown trout, rainbows, and native speckled brook trout.* Of these the rainbows are the least apt to settle down, he says—they come from a sea-running species, which is used to larger waters, and before a year is out they take off, presumably, downstream. The browns are thought to be the real stayers— their species was brought to this country from Europe, many years ago, and has proven hardy in our streams, being not too susceptible, relatively, to the lures of fishermen, and being also tough and voracious—inclined to drive competing fish away. Among those so driven, finally (from the Tilt home waters), are thought to be a number of the native brook trout planted. These mainly go upstream, it is thought—to the extent our new beaver-dams allow them—and find their way, eventually, into the smallest feeder-brooks—thus restoring the Golden Age prevailing early in this century, when our waters teemed with brookies—lively and lovely fish, but not very wary.

So the pattern is rainbows below the Tilt farm, browns dominating the Tilt home waters, and browns shifting over to natives up above. Just what the mixture is at the Miners' farm—a mile or so from the Tilts'—would be hard to say, but the volume of trout, at least, is huge there, as I have seen. I used to walk that brook in the 'thirties, and I rarely saw trout in it—often I saw only

* For more on trout see Chapter VII.

the big still suckers in the holes. But if I walk it now, and watch it, I forever see trouts' darting figures, and sometimes they are big—ten inches long or more. They dash from cover to cover in the brook—it is the width, say, of a modest dirt road. They whisk and turn on the bottom, sometimes raising a puff of mud, like a dust-puff.

Those fish must be good pickings for even so careless an otter as the one I saw. And they have brought other predators to the stream—Mr. Tilt mentions mink and herons especially (and not too happily). The Tilt stocking program must, in fact, be supporting many such predators—and increasing their numbers by enabling more of them to live past childhood.

Beavers are vegetarians, and presumably take no trout, but they get into the Tilt black books another way. When they dam the water—making it lie still in the sunshine—they raise it above the cool temperatures that trout do well in. So Mr. Tilt has been encouraging a neighbor's son to trap out a family of them, ensconced below his bridge. (Last fall, for the first time in ages, private citizens were allowed to catch beavers with steel jump-traps—the crippling kind—in Connecticut. Before that, if one had a beaver problem, one could only get a State official to come and trap them out, unharmed, with box-traps—then the official would have to find a wild, watery beaverless place to free them in, with such places growing fewer all the time.)

When I was a boy the beaver was extinct here, and conservation—plus introduction—has brought it back. Today one even hears beavers called a pest in Salisbury, though I doubt if they are all that bad. Occasionally they flood a road or a cellar here, which the humans won't tolerate. They have also cut down some artificial tree plantations, which is considered naughty. And a few of them caused trouble awhile ago at the outlet dam of Riga Lake—they blocked up the spillway; then Spalding Mc-Cabe replied by opening a sluice-gate lower down in the dam, thus dropping the lake's level; then the beavers blocked the sluice-gate too; and in the end they had to be trapped out. Otherwise—apart from the unsightliness of flood-killed trees in their bailiwicks—they do little damage, and we seem embarked on a long co-existence with them. George Kiefer, our local forester, says that beavers are a scant burden economically—the swamp-trees they flood are nearly worthless, he says, and so is their usual fodder tree, the aspen, known in Salisbury as the popple. Our deer weigh much heavier on the forests, according to George, as they consume the saplings of a really valuable tree, the sugar maple.*

I know five beaver colonies within a mile or two of my brother Jake's house—and I suspect there are more, because some beavers just live in holes in the stream-banks —they don't advertise themselves by dams and lodges. Of my five known colonies, three are multiple-dam affairs—complex arrangements of canals and ponds— which I find fascinating. I visit the beavers' places again and again, just to look at the engineering. I take friends to see them too, and I figure that the beavers have put Salisbury on almost the same level, sightseeingwise, as Manhattan, with *its* peculiar structures. The key building material of our beavers—corresponding to the human brick or timber—is a stick, perhaps of popple, somewhat longer than the human walking-cane. To make their dams and lodges, the beavers stack and weave in-

* See Chapter IV.

numerable sticks together, weighting them with stones
if necessary, and chinking them with marvelous com-
binations of mud, moss, leaves, etc. One can walk across
a beaver dam—new ones give, and are springy, but old
ones are almost like terra firma. I have pulled apart only
one lodge—in a swamp near Jake's house, where the
beavers themselves had been trapped out. There was a
snug little chamber there, and I believe its entrances
were many yards away, beneath the water. In winter, as
I understand it, when their ponds freeze over, the beavers
live a subsurface life except for the lodges themselves.
But I am no expert on this, or on the beavers' other ways.
They have entered my life in middle age, only, and it
was in childhood that I learned things.

So far we have dealt only with man's direct influence,
ecologically, but we should also touch on man's best
friend, for his ways have been changing in parallel fashion, and with parallel effect. When I was a boy the
standard Salisbury house had a dog or two around it—
sometimes a pedigreed one, but more often a mongrel.
In either case, the dogs were treated as mere dogs. They
were fed a random diet of kitchen scraps and were on
their own otherwise—were free to roam, hunt, and generally be vagabond, so long as the dog-catcher didn't get
them. Between them they chased our deer, hunted our
squirrels and rabbits, and especially kept our woodchucks down. My father's farm was an extreme case,
perhaps, but it was indicative. We usually had two dogs
on the place—perhaps one pedigreed and one mongrel—
and they roamed freely and caught woodchucks all the
time. Sometimes we boys would hear them barking far
away. We would go and find them, perhaps on the edge of

a distant field, and they would have a woodchuck in a stone wall there. We would pull the wall down, and one of the dogs would get the woodchuck by its neck and shake it to death—we had an Airedale, for many years, who could shake most fearfully. This again was a bloodthirsty business, yet it seemed part of the natural life and it certainly kept the woodchucks within bounds.

The modern dogs of Salisbury are apt, though, to live differently. Humans here live more out of tin cans now than they did then. Hence they have fewer kitchen scraps. Hence their dogs, too, live more out of cans. And hence, as canned dogfood is costly—and the cost is obvious on the grocery bill—our dogs are fewer. They are also more costly themselves, each for each, than they used to be, according to an apparent economic law—illogical as it may be—that if one pays a lot for dogfood one should pay a lot for the dog as well. So our depleted dog population has a high percentage, now, of poodles, boxers, and other fancy types, whose owners, not surprisingly, keep them at home—keep them out of the hunting-field (where their urbanity might work against performance anyway). The place across the road from my brother's, to name one example, used to be a well-dogged farm, but now it is occupied by the House of Herbs, whose proprietress, Mrs. Ezra Winter, has only a small poodle, named Jeremy, that never leaves the house unaccompanied. Of course the intervening road itself—Route 44—is much more dangerous than it used to be, which is a main reason for Jeremy's confinement. There are many reasons for these things, indeed, but most of them—so far as one can tell—derive from the machine age.

We used often to see dogs on the loose here, and now

we seldom see them. This helps explain the tameness of our deer, and perhaps that of our squirrels and chipmunks, which is considerable. Above all it explains the behavior of our woodchucks, for which outrageous seems the proper adjective. Woodchucks are seen on lawns here now; they get into people's cellars; and George Miner even says that one came up on his front porch last summer. Such acts would not have been tolerated in my boyhood. Nor is effrontery the only thing wrong with them —there is the economic side. Our town's many fields of alfalfa (itself a rather new feature here) are simply riddled nowadays with chuckholes. Our gardens are raided mercilessly by chucks, and the House of Herbs, understandably, is suffering too—Mrs. Winter says that her chervil, tarragon, and basil, especially, get rooted up. The reason for it all seems obvious: dear old unspecialized Rover has had his day. Nature abhors a vacuum, and when the dog leaves the lawn the woodchucks come up onto it.

IV. THE WOODS

LAST SUMMER I indulged a long-held wish: I lived by myself in a cabin in the woods. This sounds like Thoreau, but in truth it wasn't. My sojourn lasted two and a half months, as against his two years, and throughout it I was well supplied, by my daughter Mary, from a neighboring supermarket. Yet still I *was* alone, with the birds and trees, and I did learn something of the everchanging forest.

I learned about that locality in it, too, which is special. I was on a wooded plateau some hundred miles north of New York City—at the junction of the New York, Connecticut, and Massachusetts borders—and in the eighteenth and nineteenth centuries that region had been a center of the U.S. iron idustry. Salisbury, the township in which my cabin stood, had sometimes been called the American Birmingham in those earlier days—it had been a main source of guns and other munitions in the Revolution, the War of 1812, and the Civil War. In those days not coal, but charcoal, had been used in making iron, and my plateau had been cut over again and again to obtain it. There had been settlements on the plateau then, and many roads and other works of man. It had all stopped in the late nineteenth century, though. The woods had grown back on the scars, and that page of history is now almost forgotten. But there are traces still—in old roads, in old stonework, in peculiarities of the forest—and with the help of friends I explored these as the summer passed.

My cabin was in Connecticut, but it was just a few yards south of the Massachusetts line, a fact on which hung its existence and its availability to me. It had been built in the late nineteen-forties, as a hunting-lodge and hideaway, by two Navy enlisted men from nearby in Massachusetts. They had bought some tax-delinquent plateau woodland on the Massachusetts side and had then gone ahead, they thought, to build on this. But they had miscalculated. Their cabin had turned out to be in Connecticut, and the Connecticut landowners had asked them to move it. They had done so, reluctantly, but had miscalculated again. They had found themselves still in Connecticut and had given up the struggle, letting the owners take the cabin over for a nominal rent. And thereafter the latter, having no pressing need for the building, had lent or rented it to stray occupants like myself.

It was a substantial frame job, of only one room but spacious, with two stoves and five big windows. It stood on a bank above a cold and babbling brook, resting there on piers of concrete blocks. The blocks, stoves, windows, lumber, and everything else had been carried in over several hundred yards of rough trail, and this feat—plus of course the knocking down and moving of the whole establishment—repeatedly inspired admiration for the builders in those who came to see me. The builders were long gone by then, but meanwhile others who had used the place had improved it, partly winterizing it and equipping it with pots, pans, dishes, and a few necessary tools like saws. The cabin made an excellent pad, all in all, and it was there gratuitously, out of the blue, thanks largely to confusion over the border.

Later on, when I was drawn into studying the plateau's history, I learned that border confusion had played a big part in its early days. The plateau, which takes up about fifty square miles in the corner of the three states, is known officially as the Taconic Range (perhaps from an Indian word meaning "wild place"), but colloquially its parts are apt to have other names of their own. The Connecticut part is generally called Mount Riga, and its woodsman inhabitants, now alas a vanishing race, have long been known as Raggies. The plateau is a familiar sight to many who drive northward from New York. It stands on your right if you drive northward between Millerton and Hillsdale, or on your left if you go up from Salisbury to South Egremont, on the way to Great Barrington. From either of these sides it has a stage-drop look, as if it were but a single range of peaks, yet in fact the ranges are two, and between them lie troughs and flatland, some thousand feet above the road that you are traveling. A small part of the trough-land—in the remote township of Mount Washington, Mass.—is cultivated, but most is abandoned to forest, and the whole plateau has a Lost World quality.

The three states meet on the plateau's western side, not far from the New York hamlet of Boston Corners (so named because it was once the corner of Massachusetts or the Boston state). The present meeting-place is east of Boston Corners and higher up, on a wooden mountain. The region near that point is stable and quiet now, but it wasn't always so, according to what I have read. In Colonial times Connecticut and Massachusetts, both de-

riving from the Massachusetts Bay Colony, agreed pretty
well on their boundary, but neither agreed with New
York, which was Dutch in origin and laid out on the radically different manorial system. In the seventeenth century New York made claims lying far east of the present
border—as far as the Connecticut River—and the other
two states made ones lying still farther west—as far as
the Pacific, or whatever else might terminate the land in
that direction. In time the hostile claims were reduced,
but they weren't immediately reconciled, and the problem continued even when the Dutch were supplanted in
New York by the British.

In 1685 Robert Livingston was granted Livingston
Manor in York State, running eastward from the Hudson above Poughkeepsie. He and Philip Livingston, his
son and heir, were aggressive landlords. They had a forward policy and a constabulary of their own, and they
are said to have made life hard for people of Connecticut
or Massachusetts affiliation on and around the Taconic
Range—forcibly collecting rents from them or, failing
that, burning them out and driving off their cattle.
Bloodshed and death were common in these disputes, or
so one reads today, and the borderland township of Ancram, now in New York, was said until recently to be
haunted as a result by ghosts called the Ancram Screechers. The existence of these Screechers was well established in the folklore of the old Raggies, who said their
screams could be heard, when conditions were right, on
the plateau's Connecticut side.

In 1731 Connecticut ended its differences with New
York by a survey that has held good, with small variations, ever since. The survey gave form to a complicated
deal whereby Connecticut got the Stamford-Greenwich

panhandle—already full of Connecticut settlers—in return for the notch just above it, near Wilton, and for an
eastward move of the whole border north of that, by
"one mile, three quarters of a mile, twenty rods and five
links," into land then tentatively judged to be Connecticut territory. (In 1700 William III of England had
signed an agreement that the border should lie twenty
miles east of the Hudson. So in 1731 the surveyors came
east twenty miles from that river, toward Mount Riga,
then came farther east by the "one mile, three quarters
of a mile" etc., and then ran the border straight south,
thus taking a slice off Connecticut that was supposed to
equal the panhandle minus the notch. It made, and still
makes, an odd-looking line, but it was accepted and has
worked.)

Massachusetts was slow to follow suit, though; not till
1787 did she make her New York agreement. Even then
the line was unsound geographically. Boston Corners,
the angle of the Massachusetts border, lay almost two
miles west of Connecticut's angle—because of the slice
taken off the latter state; and besides it was down on the
lowlands to the Riga plateau's west, cut off by a steep
escarpment from the rest of Massachusetts itself. Massachusetts peace officers couldn't get into it easily, and they
were also—together with their colleagues of New York
and Connecticut—unsure of their jurisdiction in the
complexity of the borders. The corner was a virtual nomansland, where miscreants could play a game of pris-
oner's base—they called it "dodging the line." Murder-
ers, counterfeiters, and others are said to have dodged
the line there for long periods. Massachusetts ended the
anomaly in 1853 by ceding a triangle at the corner to
New York, but the lawless atmosphere prevailed there

up to that moment. On October 12, 1853, an illegal bare-knuckle fight was held at Boston Corners between John Morrissey and Yankee Sullivan. It was an age when fights often took place on rafts and other hard-to-police bits of territory, and Boston Corners filled the bill.

These facts I learned at the end of my summer, by research. At its beginning, though my cabin was little over a mile from the three-state junction, I was not mindful of such things, but was concentrating on my own comfort, or at least survival, in my new environment. Last June was cool throughout that region, and it was especially cool where I was. The whole plateau is colder anyway than the neighboring lowlands—the snow is deeper there in winter, the skating begins earlier in the fall. Then my brook, fed by springs in the stone mountains, made that part of it colder still, and above all the shade made it cold. The forest there had been cut for charcoal in the past, but it had long since grown in again (with variations that I was to learn about later). It had closed the canopy, as the foresters say, and now on the best of days it let only a few bright dapples of sunlight down onto its floor. The scene by my cabin was somewhat like those in the twilight jungles of Malaya or the Congo, and it took getting used to. In the mornings I would stay inside the cabin, writing, and then I might wear one, two, three, or even four sweaters. In the afternoons I would cut wood or do something else out of doors, and then I might get reasonably warm—if I got warm enough I would almost enjoy the quick bath I took, around tea-time, in the icy stream. In the evenings I would read for a while, comfortably enough, by the light of a Coleman lantern, and then around the late dark—

toward ten o'clock—I would go to bed. I had rigged up a sleeping-tent on the other side of the brook—it was a wall-less fly, made from a tarpaulin, with a camp cot and mosquito net beneath it. This too was cold on a cold night, and at such times I would wear sweaters to bed and would pile on whatever blankets and other warm things I had available. It was a healthy life in the long run, but one that set you back at the start—especially you failed to get the glowing tan that people nowadays link with outdoor well-being; instead you got the pallor that they link with jails.

The cabin was in a shallow gorge cut in the stone, over the ages, by the brook. The stone of that region is a blackish gray, and in many parts the plateau seems made from it entirely. Most of the area near my cabin had no true soil on it—I did eventually find a good patch of this, on a bench above the stream, and was there able to bury garbage, but I did much hunting first; it was almost like finding a vein of precious ore. The rest of the nearby ground was only a mulch, a few inches deep, made up of leaf fragments, old bark, and other organic matter. Beneath this shallow covering one hit the rock, which near the stream took the form of gravel, stones and boulders— higher up the slopes, in hydraulically less turbulent places, it came in big continuous sheets or ledges.

The mulch near the brook was a thin base indeed, yet from it, amid the shade and coolness, arose a variety of trees. The biggest and perhaps most numerous were hemlocks, the main evergreens of our region. With their dark trunks, dense shade, and almost bare brown needle-carpets, they set the tone for the somber landscape. There were also a few beeches, with silver trunks, and many red oaks, red maples, sugar maples, and yellow birches.

The oaks and maples grew to a fair height, approaching that of the biggest hemlocks. The birches, as a rule, were shorter. They would start up well, but soon their trunks would stop and splay out into smaller branches or suckers. These were a dark reddish brown, while the main trunks were gray with orange undertones. The birches' bark feathered off in silky curls, and their trunks were gnarled or muscular. Their roots might run for yards in the open—twistingly, and with the same gray bark—over the slate-colored rocks.

All these trees made their contributions to the canopy, which despite the shade it cast was usually a bright green when you looked up at it. Then beneath it, half way to the ground or so, was a scattering of saplings and "understory" trees or shrubs—holding their own, with splashes of green, wherever they could catch some sun. And finally, beneath these and near the ground itself, were ferns, tree-seedlings, and other low plants. There were few ferns near the cabin because the canopy was too dense there, but to the westward, beside the path on which I came and went, it was thinner and there was a sea of them. Ferns and canopy, between them, made for a very bright-green effect in that quarter. I have since read that Salisbury has thirty-one varieties of fern. I didn't learn any of these in my summer, but I often gazed at the ferns in a general way. Sometimes a breeze would seize one of them—a single frond out of the multitude—and set it dancing to and fro in a lively manner that ferns have. It would dance and dance, incessantly, amid the still and vegetative sea around it.

Besides all these growing things there was one big category of dead stuff: the trunks of chestnut trees, remaining from the blight of half a century ago. The woods were full of these old chestnuts, a few still upright, many half-fallen and leaning against other trees, but most lying near the ground—sometimes they lay in drifts together, like jumbled matches. The larger chestnuts were a foot through at their butt ends. They had long since lost their bark and on the outside were a nice old weathered gray, though sometimes lightly charred by a fire that had burned through there. Where rain had got into the trunks, via checks or knot-holes, they were rotted, sometimes entirely. But usually they were good still on the inside—firm and hard and dry, and colored a pinkish-yellow. I used to cut them up for firewood. Dry chestnut saws through in a clean, straightforward way and is sublimely easy to split—with slight exertion, working on it, you can feel yourself an able woodsman. The logs themselves are excellent for barbecuing—they burn easily, make a hot bed of coals, and impart a pleasant flavor. They also make good stovewood, or at least make the kind I wanted. I used only one of the cabin's two stoves, an old-fashioned Glenwood cooking-range—the other, a space-heater, served me as a desk for most of the summer. I also cooked breakfast only, as a rule, getting the other two meals up from cold things. What I needed, therefore, was something that would start fast and burn hot quickly, and the chestnut did just that. It didn't last long, but I didn't mind. If I wanted the fire to go on into the morning—for washing clothes, say—I would just keep throwing more logs on. But normally I was glad to forget it after breakfast, and let it die.

At first glance the forest seemed an unchanging, timeless thing, yet it was anything but that. If you watched it you saw that it was changing by the hour and by the day; then soon you realized that it must have been changing by the year and by the decade; and finally you knew quite well that it was always changing, always in flux, and probably always would be.

When I moved to the cabin, in mid-June, there was a plague of caterpillars on. They were a pale leaf-green and were thin and smooth and about an inch long—they were inch-worms every millimeter, indeed, for they moved in the inching way. They did while crawling, that is—they also moved vertically by the use of filaments, with which they hung from trees and other high things. They were everywhere in June, crawling or hanging, and I kept picking them off my clothes. I was in for a busy summer, I felt, yet the caterpillars vanished in a week or two, leaving no trace except for bare red oaks. They liked the red-oak leaves, and they cleaned off many trees on my part of the plateau—there was a tall oak across the brook from me, and they left it like a tree in winter.

A few weeks later there was a big hatch of small, pretty, cream-colored moths along the brook. There were clouds of them, and they too were everywhere—in the air, on the ground, and on the surface of the brook itself, where they would fall when spent. Their floating bodies gathered on the quieter pools and made an overall cream coating in some places. They were so thick that the stream's little trout—there were four of these in one pool near me, and two in another—could in no wise keep up with feeding on them. That hatch also stopped in a week or two. It was followed by a lull, and then by another prodigious hatch, of moths about the same size, but now pure white in color, like the whitest of eggshells. That hatch was smaller than the earlier one, but it lasted longer; some of its members, dainty and bridelike, were fluttering about weeks later.

Those two visitations were accompanied, off and on, by the appearance of other moths, many of them colored and patterned like dead leaves. I didn't try to identify the moths—didn't even try to learn which of them might be a later phase of the green caterpillars. I left them alone, merely trying to keep them out of my cabin in the evenings, when my lamp would set up a fatal attraction for them. If they got in then they would immolate themselves against the lamp itself or else be trapped when daylight came—they were hard to catch and liberate, for often they got between the flyscreens and glass windows, where I couldn't reach them. They would flutter out their short lives there under the eye of little spiders— hiding in nearby cracks of the carpentry—who would wait to emerge and deal them a *coup de grâce*. I didn't intervene much with the spiders either. The whole process seemed so natural—so overwhelming, with its wave after wave of life—a wave of foliage, then one of caterpillars, then a wave or two of moths, then one of trout and spiders—that I could only sit and wonder at it.

Insects troubled me little personally in the summer, perhaps because the weather was cool and dry. There were few mosquitos round the cabin, and few midges. There were some deer-flies, or horse-flies as I call them —the biting kind—but not enough to be a pest, and of house-flies there were almost none. An occasional ant came into the cabin, scouting around, but it never seemed to go and get its fellow ants; and the great terrors of the cities, such as cockroaches, were nowhere near. Perhaps the most common crawling thing, as time went on, was the daddy long-legs. A daddy might drop lightly on my brow at any time—so lightly that I couldn't tell, without reaching up, that it wasn't a breeze. All these creatures came and went, and so did others that I couldn't put a name to. They were less of a trial than a thing of interest—a passing show—in their variety.

The passing show of birds was still more interesting, to me, because less expected. When I moved in I found what I took to be a fairly stable bird population. Among others there were phoebes nesting under the cabin's eaves; there were scarlet tanagers; there was an owl nearby; there were mixed thrushes—including veeries —that sang offstage, especially toward dusk; and there was a whippoorwill that came on with its song around nine-fifteen on those late June evenings. The tanagers were a special joy—I had never known them before. There were two males and a female, the latter being different shades of green and the former a rich red (not scarlet really—not so yellow) with black wings and tail. The males were incredibly beautiful against the bright-green canopy of leaves, and the females too were beautiful. They would sit up there when I first came, gazing at me solemnly and repeating their song, which to me sounded like *tchk oeui*. They always sat broadside to me, gazing with one eye alone, and they turned by hopping and doing a complete one-hundred-and-eighty degrees. They did this stiffly, almost mechanically, which gave them a classical air, with their gorgeous plumage amid the leaves. And having turned they continued to look down, with one eye or the other, and to say *tchk oeui*.

They made the place a toyland forest, but in a few days they departed. I fear I drove them off with my noise and bustle—later on, and elsewhere, I heard other tanagers singing, but they seldom came near the cabin after that. The owl left my neighborhood too, before long, perhaps because of me, or perhaps because of some blackbirds that tormented it. The owl hung out in a hemlock stand across the brook, and twice after my arrival the blackbirds came to badger it there—that was how I learned, indeed, of its presence. The second time they got it on the run and chased it through the woods nearby, and I saw it—a thick brown figure coasting silently between the trees, while the blackbirds screamed behind it. It got back to its hemlocks that day, but it must have left soon afterward—I was aware of it, anyway, no more.

These blackbirds came by a good deal in my first few weeks. They came flying down the brook, often in the late morning—twenty or more of them, clucking and chirping and stopping to drink or to forage, aggressively, in the old leaves by the streamside. They would jostle each other, and throw their weight around, and be raucous like so many Blackshirt thugs—the woods would be deathly quiet when they came, except for the noise they made themselves. I used to fear they would drive the phoebes out, but they didn't. The phoebes stayed for weeks, my constant companions—one of them usually perching out over the stream, awaiting flies. When they finally left it was either because their young were old enough to take the road, I think, or else because the same young had come to a tragic end via some bluejays that had shown up. Either of these hypotheses—and many others, I suppose—would have fitted the timing of their withdrawal.

The bluejays, five or six of them, arrived well on in July and hung about for several weeks, being more raucous and menacing than the blackbirds even. They may,

I think, have been a setting of young birds just recently fledged. So may half a dozen robins that likewise showed up in July and stayed around. I believe many of the bird changes that I witnessed were tied to this part of the life cycle—old birds hatching their eggs and moving out, young birds maturing elsewhere and moving in. I got a clearer view of this life cycle from the grouse or partridge. There were no partridge near my cabin, but I used to see them when walking elsewhere in the woods. In June the partridge mothers were guarding their chicks; if I happened near them they would make a great fuss, scurrying away from the brood, to attract me, while feigning a broken wing or other ailment—one mother mewed uncannily, hauntingly, as she limped and scurried off. Then by mid-July the mothers were gone and the young, much larger, were on their own in coveys—I would put up eight or nine at once. And by late August they were breaking away—full grown now—as singles. They kept moving, too, as they grew older—going into less safe places—and I think the bird world was shifting this way all summer.

Other shifts, I believe, came from warfare over territory—every day there was a fight of some sort by the stream—and still others must have come from subtler causes. I didn't probe into these—I was a mere spectator, not an ornithologist—but I kept a bird-book on my writing-table, and I had a fine procession to watch. I saw chickadees feeding upside down below waving branches. I saw nuthatches working down the trunks of trees, and brown creepers working up them. I saw bright orioles and woodpeckers drop from the canopy; and once a cedar waxwing—a fantastic bird with a black mask like a highwayman's—came and looked right in the window at me. Warblers of many kinds came down from the treetops too—black-and-white warblers, among them, that seemed patterned after skunks. A catbird hung around for some time; so did a dark-brown wren; and a pair of Louisiana water-thrushes frequented the brook for weeks, flying up and down it, chirping, and wading and dipping in the water. In June I could identify few of these birds, but as time passed I grew familiar with them.

Toward summer's end the bird-life thinned, but not without new accessions. Towhees moved in numerously —their simple song came to dominate the place—and a pair of kingfishers moved in too. The kingfishers—with their rough crests, white collars, and long pointed bills —were the biggest, chestiest, and most spectacular birds, except for the owl, that I ever saw there. They sat on branches outside my window, or else they flew up and down the stream, and it resounded with their cry (like an extra-loud fishing-reel running out). Why they came only then, at the summer's end, I cannot say. Not one of the birds I had known in June was left by that time. The kingfishers came at the end of the parade. They came in grandly, and they added grandly to the sense of flux, of nature always changing while yet remaining, essentially, the same.

I don't doubt that nature's other realms—those of the mammals, say, and of the reptiles—were changing on Mount Riga too last summer, but I didn't see enough of them to tell. I was aware of them sporadically. I saw deer sometimes while walking. I saw raccoons too, and heard them at night—they would raid my garbage then, and if I left too many dirty dishes in the stream they would jangle them till I shouted at them to stop. I saw no bobcats—they are very aloof—but I heard that they were plentiful, at the moment, on the mountain. I saw no rattlesnakes either, but they were there. One, with ten rattles, was even found basking, toward the summer's end, on the Appalachian Trail, the mountain path that leads from Maine to Georgia. The Trail runs for fifteen miles on the Riga plateau—it passes a half mile from my cabin—and many hikers walk it in the summer to enjoy the wilderness. In July I was told that the rattlesnakes, being shy, had been driven far from the Trail by the hikers, but that was hardly true in this case. A young boy discovered the snake right in the Trail itself, in the stretch where the latter crosses Mount Everett in Massachusetts. And I know of two other rattlers, at least, that were found on the plateau last summer.

Interesting as these creatures were, though, they taught me little, as I say, concerning change. In the end I did better by studying man's history on Mount Riga, and its effect on the trees and other growing things. This was partly because I had good instruction from a friend, George Kiefer, and partly because the serious human occupation of the mountain—ending several decades earlier—had left clear archeological traces. These were scattered everywhere and included old wagon-roads, irregular excavations, and "pits" where charcoal had been burned. The pits were mysterious looking: level circles flush with the ground—about the size of a silo's base—with trees around their edges, but with little growing from inside them. The excavations were just holes in the ground, and the roads were old two-rutted wagon-tracks, made to haul charcoal, that had formed a big network centering on Riga Village, a once bustling community, now defunct, three miles to my cabin's south.

The old roads were in differing states of repair. One was even motorable—a dirt road traversing the plateau from south to north. Others had been obliterated, for long stretches, by laurel and second growth. And still others were in between—were kept open as wood-roads, without improvement, for logging or other uses. The Appalachian Trail followed such roads for much of its course on the plateau, and its habitués kept them cleared. I used to walk down the Trail on Saturdays, to visit my brother in Salisbury, and for miles I would go on a nice old wood-road along the plateau's east escarpment. The road was well laid; it was built up by stonework in the marshy places; and once, where it crossed a stream, it had the remains of good stone bridge piers left. I was curious, naturally, about the roads and the charcoaling, and in time I asked George Kiefer, a forester who looks after those woods, to help explain it all to me.

He agreed, and we set out one morning on a charcoal road not far to my cabin's south—a good one, still in use for lumbering. We were talking, luckily, and didn't walk too fast—George is a tall man, in his late thirties, and has a name for setting a stiff pace in the woods. He is a well-educated forester, having done graduate work at Duke University, but he also likes the tramping end, and he likes the old-time woodsmen and their lore—he gets his knowledge from all these sources.

We followed the road a few hundred yards, and then it went right through a charcoal pit. To me the pit looked mysterious as usual—a bare circle in the midst of nowhere—but George began explaining it. First he paced it off. "It's twenty-four feet in diameter," he said. "That's about average, though sometimes they are bigger—they can be thirty-five." He knelt and dug in the ground a moment, then came up with a small piece of charcoal in his hand. It must have been there for many decades, but it was still jet black and it looked like coal from a fire of this year. "Charcoal doesn't change much," George went on. "In the old days they used it to mark boundaries in the Plains states, if there weren't any stones around. They would dig a hole and put charcoal there, and that would be a lasting record." He bent and got another coal from elsewhere in the circle. "That's how it is," he said. "These pits have charcoal all over them—pieces that were too small to rake up after the burning. Since they don't change they give no nourishment to vegetation, and then the burning itself has cooked the organic matter out of the soil below. That's why so little grows here now."

But a few things did well on the old pits, he added. Aspens, called popples in Salisbury, did well enough, and so did laurel—where you found thick laurel in the woods, George explained, the chances were that fire had burned there in the past and given it a head start—if not a charcoal fire, then an unplanned forest fire. (As he spoke I remembered such forest fires from my boyhood. They had raged often on Mount Riga in those days, and I remembered the men of Salisbury going up there, with shovels, to fight them. And then last summer, earlier, I had been through big expanses of laurel on the mountain, where the canpoy was thin, and these must have been linked with those old blazes. The laurel had been hard to walk through, but beautiful, especially in June, when blooming, with its pink-white flowers amid its dark-green leaves.)

George told me how the old charcoal-burners, the colliers, had made their pits. First they had cleared and leveled off their circle, he said, then they had taken some four-foot logs and leaned them together in its center, making a cone or tepee-shape. Next they had taken more logs and leaned them outside this, widening the pile and keeping it circular, till they had reached the pit-base's rim. Then on that storey of logs they had put another, its diameter smaller, and then another and another, till they had had a solid pile of dome or beehive shape. Each pile had taken thirty or forty cords of wood, and they had covered it, when finished, with leaves and with a coating, several inches thick, of dirt—the leaves to keep the dirt from sifting down among the logs, the dirt itself to damp the burning. They had dug the dirt from the little excavations, here and there, that still remained—they had scratched it up wherever they could find it. They had moved it to the pit on wheelbarrows that had had huge wheels, George told me—four feet in diameter—for negotiating the rough ground.

The colliers had always left some tinder in the beehive's center, on the ground, and when ready they had fired it through a channel from the outside. George said the channel had run horizontally from the beehive's outer base; others, later in the summer, told me it had run down from the apex like a chimney. Either way, at any rate, the igniting fire had passed through it; the tinder had caught; and from then on the problem had been to control the burning, a lengthy process. "It might take the pit a week and a half to burn," George told me, "and then another week to cool. Sometimes it took twenty-five days altogether. The cooling period was vital. If the pit was opened too fast it might burst into flames, and that would be disastrous. The trick was to keep it smoldering, not burning, and the colliers did that by putting dirt on or scraping it away. Fire moves toward a source of oxygen, so they could guide it here and there by opening vents."

The pits had not been stable, apparently, while burning. Usually they had settled a bit, and sometimes they had puffed out in places, from internal gases. The colliers had been able to walk on them, but this had had its risks. I heard stories last summer, though not from George, of a man and a boy who had fallen through the tops of coal pits, into cavities opened up by faulty burning, and been consumed by flames there. Any sudden contact of burning charcoal with fresh air had had violent results—more than one person told me, last summer, that pits had "exploded" when that happened.

The burning pits had been checked repeatedly, both night and day, and for this the colliers had lived in shanties near them. Sometimes they had lived alone, sometimes with other colliers, sometimes with their families —George knew one old lady in our region, he said, who had been born in a coal shanty. The work seemed lonely as I looked back at it—colliers silently walking round their pits at all hours and in all weathers (they hadn't burned the coal in winter, though—in some cases the same men had cut wood in winter and burned in summer; in others there had been separate crews of cutters and colliers; but even then, apparently, the latter had knocked off in the snowy season). And I imagined how bleak the landscape on the mountain must have been then—how different from the woods I knew. I imagined great wastes of stumpland, with the gray rock often showing and with the rude dirt-covered mounds standing here and there, their flameless smoke arising in the emptiness.

The cutters and colliers, I had always heard, had drunk a good deal when they could afford it, or they had chewed gum opium, a narcotic then available. I remembered hearing about gum opium in my boyhood—a Salisbury doctor had still been prescribing it then, in the nineteen-twenties, for old colliers and other mountaineers—old Raggies—who had become addicts. The Raggies had lived a wild life on the mountain in the charcoal days, by all accounts—close to nature, such as that had been amid the stumps. They had lived in their lonely shanties on the charcoal roads, going back on them now and then to Riga Village, for company and more supplies, and then returning to cut their wood and burn their pits again. The charcoal too had gone out on those roads, much of it to an iron-furnace—still standing now—in Riga Village itself. Later last summer I looked into Riga Village, and into the Raggies, and into the iron industry their charcoal had served. But now I was concentrating on the landscape.

When we had seen enough of the coal pit George and I moved on. We walked through woods that were thinner, by a good deal, than those in my ravine, and that had more low-lying greenery in them. George began talking about their history. The virgin forest on the mountain had prevailed, he told me, till some time after the coming of the white man. Then the charcoal burning had begun, and after that everything sizeable, with one exception, had been cut off again and again. "They came through each thirty-five years," said George, "and cut what had grown since the last time—the trees would be several inches thick then, making the labor worth their while. They would cut off the hardwood, that is— the deciduous trees—but they would leave the hemlock because it made poor charcoal. Hemlock bark was used for tanning in those early days, and there were tanneries in this region, but it can't have paid to send Mount Riga bark to them. So the hemlocks were left standing here, and I could show you any number that are a hundred and thirty or a hundred and forty years old. I have often checked the age of such trees, after they have been cut, by counting their annual rings. And the rings will also tell you, sometimes, when the surrounding woods were cut for charcoal. You will get a series of narrow rings, meaning that the hemlock was crowded in by other trees —not doing well—then suddenly, outside of these, you will get wide rings, meaning it had good access then to sun and soil. With some trees more than one cutting will be recorded in the rings. We call those old trees 'hemlock standards.' They are fine to look at, but often they are over age for lumber—they are getting rotten on the inside."

In the first cutting for charcoal, George said, there must have been a great variety of wood used, but after that there had been a predominance of chestnut—often pits had been made up eighty per cent of chestnut wood. "That's because it grew back fast," he explained. "Not from seeds, but from shooting or suckering off the old stumps. The chestnut shoots would dominate the new growth when the next cutting fell due, thirty-five years later. They might be a foot through then, at breast height, and green chestnut cuts like butter. The cutters did all their work with axes—they didn't need saws in that young growth." Intensive cutting of the mountain had ceased in the late nineteenth century—most parts had not been cut since 1885, according to George. Then the chestnut blight had struck around 1915, killing the trees that still lay in the forest. "But in the long run the chestnuts would have thinned out anyway," George told me, "because while they shoot fast from the old stumps, they are not tenacious as a species. They have not been prominent in the ultimate forest—the climax forest, we call it—in this latitude."

Like other laymen, perhaps, I had always thought that if you cut down a virgin forest it would grow back again, straight off, with much the same make-up as before. This isn't true at all, George explained to me. "There is a regular series of growth," he said, "that follows when cleared land is left to itself. First you get fast-growing things that crave lots of sunlight and have good seed-dissemination—or that shoot readily from stumps like the chestnuts. Then come slower things that can tolerate more shade, and after them more tolerant ones still. Around Salisbury it works about like this. First you get goldenrod and hardhack—the low growth of deserted fields. Then, pushing up through this, come certain of the scrubbier trees—gray birch, for instance, and white pine. These volunteers, as we call them, prepare the seed-bed and the microclimate—the shade and so on—for what comes later. The next species may be red maple in these parts, and then in the long run it is joined—perhaps supplanted—by sugar maple, hemlock, beech, the oaks, the ashes, and yellow birch. It takes about three hundred years to achieve the climax forest here—the forest will vary from place to place, according to soil and moisture, but it will be very stable in character and will be dominated by shade-tolerant trees like hemlock. Hemlock has few equals for staying-power in this latitude. When it is established almost nothing but fire will get it out. It is far more tenacious than the other evergreens —than white pine, for instance. If you find a stand of white pine here, it probably grew from a pasture—the cattle grazed away the rival seedings, but left the pine alone, giving it a big advantage. Then finally it closed the canopy and could hold its own."

The climax forest of Salisbury—two centuries in the future now, at best—will be dark and gloomy, according to George. And early travelers used terms like that in describing the forest primeval of our township—they referred to "the forest dank and unending" and spoke of letting light, by cutting trees, into the dismal swamp. (The woods by my cabin, I must say, were approaching this state last summer. But many of the hemlocks there, according to George, were old standards—a hundred years of age or better—and besides the cabin's site, in the cool damp ravine, was one to encourage climax trees like yellow birch and hemlock itself. I was enjoying, I gathered, a localized near-preview of climax conditions—the woods on higher ground around me were much thinner.)

On a former occasion George had told me that the deer of Salisbury, which are numerous, were having a bad effect on the woods. Now, as we walked, he elaborated on this, explaining that deer browse heavily on the seedlings of economically valuable trees, like oak, ash, and maple, while almost ignoring those of beech, which is a poor market species in our region (because it "checks, bends, cups and warps" while drying). If left to them-

selves, George said, the deer might shape a new climax forest where beech would outnumber the other, better hardwoods. He showed me evidence of their work as we went along. He showed me maple seedlings, for instance—knee-high infant trees—that had little more than twig-stumps left on them, where the deer had nipped the leaves off. And he showed me other seedlings whose twigs were all disfigured, where they had been browsed, by joints and bends in their regeneration. I could see such damage everywhere, too, once George had called my attention to it. "In the virgin forest," he said, "the deer were much less plentiful than now, because they had less small growth to browse on—the green was nearly all up in the canopy. In times of heavy charcoal-burning they did badly too—their feed and cover were kept down. But in times of undisturbed new growth they have done very well, on seedlings. We are in such a time now—have been in it for decades—and besides our deer are strongly protected by the law. They breed fast, and their numbers shoot up under these conditions."

As a forester, George thought we humans were too lenient with the deer in our game laws—thought that they and we were in competition for use of the good trees, and that we gave them too much advantage in this. Walking along, he pointed to another browsed-off seedling. "Nip, nip, nip," he said. "A snowshoe rabbit may possibly have done that, but the odds are a hundred to one it was a deer."

He showed me many things that morning, all in all, and told me about many things—about the uses of the wood from the different trees, for instance, about the trees' geographical ranges, and about the damage that trees on Mount Riga have suffered from ice storms (at their tops) and forest fires (at their bottoms). But these things have little to do with charcoaling and its aftermath, and I shan't go into them here. We walked a lot that morning on old coal roads that had been reopened for lumbering. "Loggers generally pick out and use the old roads," George said, "because they so often follow the best route. Sometimes they are too narrow or too steep for modern machinery, but on the whole they are very good. The charcoal men planned them well and laid them well. They had time to do things right in those days."

On that note we parted, and I went back to my cabin in the shade. I gazed with new interest at the woods there, so like the virgin forest of the colonists. The red-oak tree, denuded by the caterpillars, stood across the brook in all its nakedness. It looked like a dead tree, and till that morning I had almost thought it that. But George had told me I was wrong. "It won't grow much this summer," he had said. "It may have no annual ring to mark this year. But that's all. Next year it will put out leaves again and keep on going."

I had asked him, too, about the yellow birches near me —why their trunks had grown no taller, why their branches splayed so at the tops. That, he had said, was no doubt because Salisbury was in the southern limit of their range. They liked a colder climate. They could get by in my ravine, with its chill and dampness, and could get by too in the climax forest. But they couldn't do much more than that—you couldn't expect them to be perfect, as in Maine or Canada.

I looked at the oak and the birches and thought about them. Then later I took a saw and went to cut some firewood. I found an old dead chestnut; and the saw, as usual, went briskly through it. And other dead chestnut trees were lying there—the place had always seemed to me a chestnut cemetery. But George had rid me of that idea as well. Chestnut suckers, he had explained, were still shooting up from the old stumps—even from the old dead trunks. He had shown me such suckers, with their long green chestnut leaves; and now, being informed, I could find them too, even in my graveyard. The suckers didn't grow very tall, George had said—the blight was still around and would kill them at an early stage. But still there were developments. One chestnut shoot on Mount Riga, the year before, had produced actual burrs with actual chestnuts in them—the first in nearly fifty years. And so there was hope and progress—life in the most dead-seeming places.

I thought about that too, as I brought my wood back, and split it, and stacked it by the stove. Then I took my dip in the brook, got dressed again, and had dinner in the gathering dusk. Thrushes sang outside—liquidly, melodiously—but the whippoorwill had ceased by then, like the tanagers. I reflected on such changes, and wondered what the birds and insects thought of them. They thought nothing, I decided. They could have no concepts —no concepts of the chestnut blight, or of the charcoal days, or of the growth potential of the leafless oak. They didn't think about these things, but they acted on them, automatically and vigorously—usually, it seemed, without knowing they were acting on them. Man's ways changed, and the woods changed. The insects changed, and the birds changed. And the animals changed too. They all adapted—they could adapt to anything. But they did it with the native hue of action, not with thought.

V. THE IRON

My cabin home of last summer—on the plateau where join the New York, Connecticut, and Massachusetts borders—was especially near two features of that height, called Bear Mountain and Sage's Ravine. The brook by my cabin fed into the latter. The brook itself was small; I could nearly step across it, and its trout seemed rarely to grow beyond five inches long. Yet Sage's Ravine, a half mile lower, to the east, was a big and awesome thing, with falls and rapids plunging into deep, dark pools—creating a moist, mysterious, cool atmosphere in the shade of ancient hemlocks. One imagined that the stream had been working there forever, wearing down the stone. In the Ravine's upper part the water was baffled again and again by rocks, but lower down it fell more sharply—so steeply that one could hardly follow it on foot. In that lower part it had cut a deep magnificent V-shaped gorge; it was, in fact, still cutting it, for the gorge's sides were lined with avalanches, with fallen —undermined—old trees, and with wild new growth arising in their places. The Ravine followed the Connecticut-Massachusetts line and made a thorough division between those states—more distinct, by far, than political boundaries elsewhere in that wilderness. And also, dropping swiftly a thousand feet, it linked the heights to the lowlands stretching off around them.

Bear Mountain, the other nearby feature, rose steeply to the Ravine's south—the brook-bank climbing past my cabin went on upward, at a good angle, to join the mountain's flank. The mountain's summit was a dome of rock, which throughout my childhood, and much earlier, had always been called the highest point in Connecticut. That honor had since been stripped away by some debunking surveyor, who had pronounced a nearby hillside, rising into Massachusetts, a few feet higher where it crossed the border. Yet still Bear Mountain *looked* higher than that other point, and it was far grander and had a better view. It also boasted a monument, a big tower of dark stones tapering inward, like Tibetan architecture, as it rose. The tower, which could be seen for miles in all directions, bore a plaque saying it stood on Connecticut's "highest ground" and had been built in 1885 by a certain Owen Travis. Early in the summer Owen Travis was just a name to me, but later I found that he had been a celebrated mason in the nineteenth-century community, long since vanished, on that plateau.

I used to go up on Bear Mountain, sometimes to pick huckleberries, sometimes merely to get the sunlight denied me, round my cabin, by the canopy of trees. The mountaintop was sparse and open—big stone ledges with pockets, now and then, of dirt and organic matter. The wind could blow hard up there; the sun could beat down; and often the soil, resting so thinly on the bedrock, would be parched. Only the smallest of trees—scrub oak, pitch pine, and small gray birches—grew there. The pines, especially, were distorted by the wind—leaning, as in a

Japanese garden, with their neat round needle-clusters—
emerald green—disposed artistically on their limbs. The
wind would sigh in the little pines as I walked near
them, and all around I would have a feeling of space. On
a good day I could see the Catskills, thirty miles away
across the Hudson. I could see up into Vermont. I could
all but see New York and Boston. Those places would
be off on the horizon. Then short of them, down below
me, would lie the open farmland of Dutchess, Litchfield,
and Berkshire counties. And short of that, again, would
be the plateau on which Bear Mountain stood—it was
a rolling woodland, green and spongy-looking, with
other knobs rising from it here and there—all smoothly
rounded, like the curves of a Maillol nude.

A veritable sea it was of woodland—its green leaves
the drops of water—yet it hadn't always been that way.
In the nineteenth century the plateau had been defor-
ested, again and again, for charcoal; and also in that
century it had bustled with an iron industry. The iron
turned out there had been rated among the world's best;
it had been favored especially for gunmetal and ship-
fittings—the anchors of the *Constitution* and its sister
ship, the *Constellation*, had been forged there on the
heights. The furnace that had smelted the iron was still
standing last summer—I passed it often, three miles to
my cabin's south—but it had not smudged the plateau
air (according to some reports) since 1847, when the
molten iron had reputedly "frozen" in its hearth, forming a "salamander" that the owners had not thought
worth while removing. I remembered the furnace, a
handsome old ruin, from my childhood. It had then been
crumbling away and had been deemed unsafe to climb
on, but then just recently—in 1961—it had been reno-

vated by a local mason, Peter Brazzale, with the backing of a local philanthropist; and so now it was a monument.

It was a rugged, archaic-looking block of masonry, thirty feet high, according to the records, and thirty by twenty-four feet at its base. It was made of the dark local stone put together without mortar, and on two of its faces there were openings, one for letting the molten iron out. These were in the shape of "false" arches; each had been built, that is, by merely sloping its two sides together till a broad stone lintel could be placed on top to join them. The work looked primitive, partly because of these false arches, yet at the same time strong and massive, like much prehistoric architecture in the Old World. Originally the masonry had been held together, in a precautionary way, by wooden beams and iron tie-bars. In the restoration the beams had been replaced by old telephone poles, running across the different faces, and these, for all their size, looked properly to scale. The whole structure in its loneliness—it stood beside a mountain brook near a dirt mountain road—was an impressive, enigmatic reminder of the past.

While camping on the plateau I had already learned something of the old charcoal-burning there, and now I began to study the iron business, which had combined with it to make the heights, now such a wilderness, into a hive of industry. I could find no one alive, of course, who remembered 1847, but I did find some documents on the iron—pamphlets and articles written by metallurgists or local historians. Also I found one local historian in person: the late Julia Pettee, then aged 90, who was descended from a Mount Riga iron-master, who had long been a professional librarian, and who had done much research on the old Salisbury—she was still doing it, in fact, last summer. I began consulting Miss Pettee and the documents, and from them I pieced together this story.

Iron-making began early in America. The technique, used in Europe for centuries, was known to the colonists, and they vitally needed its fruits—needed nails, horseshoes, pots, pans, muskets, farm tools, and other ironware. Besides this they had an export market, in England, because iron-making in those days used charcoal —lots of it—and the British forests were hard pressed. So American leaders promoted the industry from early times. By 1647 or 1648 John Winthrop, Jr., son of the Massachusetts governor, had two blast-furnaces going near Boston. The same John Winthrop became governor of Connecticut in 1657, and a year later he built a furnace just east of New Haven. Throughout the next century other furnaces went up in Massachusetts, Connecticut, and elsewhere on the Atlantic seaboard. The ore they smelted was apt to be indifferent—often it was "bog ore" dredged up from nearby ponds—but something useful could always be made from it.

Not until 1732 was ore discovered in Salisbury. The Salisbury region, at the meeting of the three states, had been slow in getting settled because it was at the end of the line from wherever one approached it. If one approached from New York one would go up the Hudson to Livingston Manor, well above Poughkeepsie, and then travel eastward to the farthest edge of the Livingston domain—to a nomansland, indeed, where the Livingstons were virtually at war with the New Englanders. And if one approached from Boston or New Haven one would go southwest or northwest, as the case might be, to the limits of civilization as conceived of in those centers. The Salisbury corner was known in Connecticut as the Western Lands or the Greenwoods, and when its iron was discovered it was inhabited only by Indians, one English colonist, and a few Dutch families who had come in from the Hudson. The iron seems to have sped up Salisbury's development, indeed, rather as the Gold Rush sped up California's.

In my researches I have come on several encomiums of the Salisbury ore: it was "as good as any found in the United States"; it was "the richest this side of Sweden"; it was "perhaps unexcelled in the world, according to the Smithsonian Institute." I have also heard it praised by Salisbury neighbors who know something about it. There may be an element of local pride in these judgments, yet it does seem that Salisbury iron had outstanding qualities—especially it must have had durability under repeated shock, for it was highly prized for guns and, later on, for railroad car-wheels. The news of its discovery, in 1732, is said to have traveled fast and far— even to Europe—but the ore was not exploited in much quantity at first, perhaps because Salisbury lacked even wagon-tracks then to link it with the outside world. Pack-horses would presumably have taken any exported ore— or iron or ironware—to the Hudson, the closest navigable waterway, which was twenty-odd miles distant as the crow flies. So only small forges or "bloomeries" were used at first, these beating out objects in scant volume.

Then in 1762 a real blast-furnace, comparable to the later Mount Riga one, was built in a part of Salisbury township that is now called Lakeville, but was called Furnace Village through the early nineteenth century. The furnace—it has since disappeared—was built by

three entrepreneurs, one being Ethan Allen, a Connecticut man who later moved to Vermont and led the Green
Mountain Boys there. They placed it near the outlet of
Lake Wononscopomuc or Lakeville Lake, where there
was a good fall of water to power the blast. In the decade
after its launching the enterprise had its ups and downs,
and it changed hands more than once. Ethan Allen sold
out in 1765, to a partner, and was fined shortly afterward
for beating the latter up (Allen, a big, irrepressible man,
soon to be a famous guerrilla, was in repeated trouble
during his Salisbury phase). When the Revolution began
the furnace was controlled by a Tory sympathizer, who
sailed off to England, after which it was taken over by
the Connecticut authorities on behalf of the war effort.
They kept it busy overtime making iron for munitions,
especially cannon. Salisbury was well placed as an ar-
senal of democracy, being fairly safe from attack, but
also near important war theaters like the Upper Hudson Valley, where Burgoyne was campaigning in 1777.
Many workmen came to Furnace Village from elsewhere, and many hogsheads of rum were brought in to
keep them going. Cannon were made here by pouring
molten iron into a cast—of clay, straw, rags, and other
materials—that was set nose up in the ground with
tamped sand around it. The moulding produced a solid
chunk of cannon shape that, when cool enough, was
taken to a nearby shed for boring. There it was hung
under the roof, muzzle down, and lowered till it came
into contact with an erect drill turned by a horse walking round and round it—the weight of the gun itself,
gradually lowered, supplied the pressure for the boring.
Later the finished gun would be fired at a nearby hill
for testing, and many cannon-balls have since been

found embedded in this hill, which is now covered by houses, a school, and an undertaking parlor.

Other munitions made at Lakeville during the Revolution included mortars, grenades, swivel-guns, and camp-kettles. An iron chain was stretched across the Hudson during the war, as a defense against British ships, and Salisbury ore was used in it; but, according to Miss Pettee, the smelting and fabricating were done elsewhere. (The British seized this chain, incidentally, and later took it to Gibraltar, where they used it for protecting the moles.)

Mount Riga, the plateau of my obsession, played only a minor part in these early events. A small forge was built there in the late eighteenth century, and Miss Pettee believed that charcoal was being burned on the heights as early as 1750. But the place was too remote, still, for big-time war industry; and then when peace came, as so often happens, doldrums came with it. The colonial furnace capacity had been expanded in the war, and now there was an industrial pause while the new states argued about their unity. It was not till 1810 that the furnace was built on Mount Riga, and even today one meets with doubts on the wisdom of its placement there. The question must have been nicely balanced. A furnace in those days needed to be in touch with five things: water-power, charcoal, iron ore, limestone, and, of course, a market for its output. In one recent pamphlet, by a metallurgist, I have read that water-power was the governing consideration, and Mount Riga scored high in that regard; it had two lakes, the upper feeding into the lower, and the lower into the dashing brook near which the furnace was built. The site was also good for charcoal—with many square miles of almost level wood-land at its door—but for ore and limestone it was poorer. Five main ore-beds were discovered eventually in Salis-bury, the greatest being at Ore Hill on the present Route 44, between Lakeville and Millerton, N.Y. All these mines were near Mount Riga, but near its base only, and the ore had to be carried upward a thousand feet in alti-tude and three or four miles in ground distance; in the beginning at least this too was done by pack-horses on mountain trails. It was the same for the limestone, except that this had to be carried still farther across the low-lands. And finally, of course, the finished products had to come down off the mountain to be sold, though some writers have called this an advantage. Once wagon-roads got developed, these writers say, the teams transporting ironware or pigs could get a flying start—a first few miles of easy, downhill hauling—toward such far objec-tives as the Hudson.

Anyway the furnace *was* built on the mountain, and it boomed there in the early nineteenth century, a period when Eastern industry was developing fast (if mainly by the old techniques) and the West was still wild and re-mote—the Erie Canal was not opened till 1825, when Mount Riga's furnace was in mid-career. The furnace was a bridge, in a way, between the colonial and modern technologies—or it was a vestige of the former on the brink of modern times—and to study it helps one under-stand that changeful moment in our history.

The furnace, then as now, was but a stone's throw from the dam of the lower Mount Riga lake, and in be-tween stood a water-wheel that drove a huge pair of leather bellows (long since vanished) to supply the blast. Then downstream, a few score yards below the furnace, was another dam (its crude remains are still there) that supplied blast air, and perhaps motive power, for secondary installations, principally two forges. I have read that these works, all together, "blazed for half a mile along the stream," which today is only a babbling sylvan affair. The old furnace—then as now—stood several yards from the stream itself, up a slope to its south; and behind it, still more southerly, rose—and rises—a considerable hill. On this hill lived most of the furnace workers, and on it were stored the operation's raw materials. The charcoal, brought in on wagons from the surrounding plateau, was kept in sheds for dryness, while the ore and limestone were stockpiled in the open. Then from that stockpile area a ramp led out northward to the furnace, and over it repeated batches of the ore, the lime, and the charcoal were carried—some writers say by horse-carts, some by man-pushed wheelbarrows—to be dumped into the smelting process.

Though block-shaped on the outside the furnace had a vertical cavity within that was cylindrical save for bulging a good deal in the middle. The cylinder's narrow top was relatively cool, and it was here that the materials were dumped. They then descended gradually, heating and mixing the while, through the broad midriff (it was sixteen feet in diameter) and into the narrow bottom, which was called the hearth. The blast of fresh air, forced by the bellows, came in, from the side, near the hearth's top and promoted intense burning there. The charcoal fueled this and supplied carbon to the iron; the limestone supplied other ingredients and also drew off certain impurities from the ore. Then in time the good molten iron collected down in the hearth while the impurities, also in liquid form, floated on top of it. These would be drawn off at their level—to cool eventually and become slag—and the metal would be tapped at intervals, by the opening of a door in the hearth, to flow out into moulds on the slope below.

It was vital, I have read, that the mixture keep moving down through the bulging cylinder, and one danger was that the hunks of charcoal, ore, and limestone would jam there and form an arch. If this happened the arch had to be broken quickly, say by poking from above, before the molten stuff lower down, supporting it, was withdrawn. Otherwise the arch might crash destructively into the emptiness, or it might simply stay there, becoming more solid all the time, and make it necessary to rebuild the furnace. Another danger was that the ore—through, say, failure of the blast—might cool in the hearth: might "freeze" there and form a salamander, as such plugs of congealed iron were called. This too would make rebuilding necessary (or abandonment, as possibly in the case of Mount Riga). And then a third danger, less to the furnace than the workers, was from the noxious gases generated in the smelting. To cope with this the gases were drawn off, upward through a vent, where they continued burning, torchlike, in the air. By day this torch "was suspended over the furnace top like a mystical oriflamme," I have read in a description of one old furnace, "and at night it served as a beacon, lighting up the countryside." It must have been a gorgeous sight, and so must the tapping of the hearth itself, which was apparently done by dark sometimes—one can imagine the blazing metal come raging and roaring out then on the primitive mountaintop.

It raged out into main-stem channels called sows and thence into side ones called pigs, which nosed up to the former like piglets to their nursing mother (thus the phrase pig-iron was born). The moulds were of sand, with enough clay mixed in to keep them shapely, but not enough so they would bake into tile under the hot metal. There was water in the mixture too, but again not enough to cause a steam explosion—the whole pig-and-sow area, in fact, was roofed over to keep out rain water, which might have had the same effect. The hot iron ran through the sows into the pigs, guided by attendants called puddlers. Then it cooled into usable bars, but not without picking up sand in the process. Most materials handled at the furnace were weighed in gross tons of 2240 pounds, but the pigs were weighed in ones of 2268, the extra twenty-eight pounds being a sand allowance.

Mount Riga was able to process about half of its pig-iron to a further stage in the two forges downstream from the furnace. One forge made big things like anchors, cauldrons, and plows. The other made "chains, garden and farm tools, hinges, latches, kitchen utensils and miscellaneous small wares." Pig-iron was also further refined into standard bars that were shipped off to fabricators elsewhere. Many bars went to the U.S. arsenals at Harper's Ferry and Springfield, Mass., to be used for musket barrels. The Springfield bars traveled all the way —sixty miles—by team and wagon. Those for Harper's Ferry were teamed over to the Hudson and went on down by tow-boat. Other bars were sent to the Collins axe company, at Collinsville near Hartford, and still others to a scythe-factory then in business on the Salisbury lowlands, near where Sage's Ravine comes down. There was a settlement there called Hammertown—in honor of the scythe industry's clangs and bangs—but those noises have long been stilled and the settlement itself has vanished.

Products of the Mount Riga forges, or of others contemporary with them, can still be seen in Salisbury. The late Mr. Joe Pickert, for instance, near the former Hammertown, had an old monkey-wrench that looked almost like modern sculpture; it had a curved, roughly beaten handle about three feet long and a simple, ingenious method of adjustment. Mrs. George Haas has a puddler's tool that looks like a massive, long-handled frying-pan. Some of the old cauldrons are still around too. One stands, as a watering-trough, on the mountain road near the old furnace. Another serves as a mammoth geranium pot outside the Haases' motel, the Ironmaster's Lodge, near Lakeville. The cauldron on the mountain is about three feet across and is round-bodied, thick, and heavy—rusty too now, of course. Those cauldons were used, among other things, for army camp-kettles, for soap-making, and for the rendering of whale-blubber. Whaling boats worked out of the Hudson in the early nineteenth century—basing, say, at Poughkeepsie—and they often carried Salisbury kettles, mounted atop brick stoves, out on their decks. They would cook their blubber while at sea.

The most notable Riga forgings were probably the anchors. Anchors of the superior Salisbury iron were used not only by the *Constitution* and *Constellation*, but by many other ships, including two frigates built in New York for the Greeks in their war of liberation (the Salisbury ironmakers sent the Greeks a big case of muskets too). The anchors were tested on the mountaintop by being hoisted on tripods and then dropped to the ground

—if they survived this they were pronounced O.K. and would be dragged off to the Hudson (each by six oxen in the early days). If the anchors were for the U.S. navy, officers would travel to Mount Riga to observe the testing; and some writers have concluded that gay, lavish balls must have been held there on these occasions. I have found no other evidence for such balls, though, and I suspect that what might be called the Ozymandias or Jamshyd convention of ruin treatment has been at work here.

> They say the lion and the lizard keep
> The courts where Jamshyd gloried and drank deep.

Mount Riga is well fixed for the lion and the lizard—in the form of bobcats and rattlesnakes—but the courts of Jamshyd take imagining. The best documented old splendor I have detected in the Riga community was embodied in its general store, which reputedly had four clerks and was better stocked, with items brought back by team from the Hudson, than were the lowland villages round about. If a Salisbury woman wanted a silk dress, I have read, she had to go up on the mountain to get it. That is hardly Jamshyd, yet it is a far cry from the lonely peace of the townsite today.

Some half dozen old houses do still remain on Mount Riga, chiefly on the hill above the furnace. Deserted in winter, they are used as summer camps by families drawn to the lake. Without maintenance by such families they would have surely gone the way, by now, of the other houses there, which have left nothing behind but old foundations and cellar-holes, perhaps with half-wild lilacs or apple-trees near by. If one prowls around the site, as I have done, one finds many of these traces—

finds evidence of an extensive settlement, including a
fair amount of open farmland, this now delineated by
old stone walls in the forest. I have read that the vil-
lagers grew wheat, flax, rye, and potatoes in the days of
the furnace. They must have also raised garden vegetables and kept pigs, chickens, and cows. But the mountain's soil is thin and its growing season short; they must
have turned to the lowlands for many things.

I have been told, I think reliably, that there were some
fifty houses in Riga Village or near it on the plateau. I
have also read that a new school built there in 1820 took
care of seventy-one pupils. And the late Phil Warner, a
devotee of the mountain, said that he heard Mrs. Thurs-
ton, one of the old inhabitants, tell his mother in the
early 1900s—at age about eighty—how she had often
looked out of her window, long ago, and seen two hundred men on the way to work. These things suggest a
population of several hundred souls, if not a thousand. It
seems likely that men predominated in the community
—such a boom town in so rough surroundings—and this
is further indicated by the presence of two extra large
foundations near the furnace, which probably, I am told,
supported boarding-houses. Many of the Riga men—the
Raggies—were good hunters and fishermen, and their
own life was probably on the wild side too. I have read
about one temperance meeting in Riga Village, after
which all the liquor in the store was thrown into the
stream. But no doubt it was soon replenished. There was
a big payroll on the mountain in boom times, and Salisbury men have always thought liquor a good investment.

The derivation of Mount Riga's name, and that of
Riga Village, is a puzzle. Catherine Maria Sedgwick, a
mid-nineteenth-century novelist of nearby Stockbridge,

Mass., wrote a moralistic tale about a young Raggy called *The Boy of Mount Righi*. She said the eminence had been named, by Swiss immigrants living there, after a Mount Righi in their own country. Miss Julia Pettee, on the other hand, has said it was named after the Baltic Riga by Latvian and Russian immigrants who had come to the mountain as charcoal-burners—she cited a tradition in her family to this effect. However, there are no Swiss, Latvian, or Russian names in the old Riga Village cemetery, nor do the Raggy descendants on the Salisbury lowlands have such names. Without exception their nomenclature seems to be English, Dutch, and French—the last reflecting, no doubt, a southward drift of Canadian woodsmen. The Raggies seem, in fact, to have had colonial blood of unexcelled purity, and the name Riga presumably has another explanation. It might, one supposes, be a back-formation from the word Raggy itself. If poor charcoal-burners were living on the mountain as early as 1750, which Miss Pettee believed, there must have been ample time, in the next century, for them to get the name Raggy and their domain that of Ragga. Riga can still be pronounced almost Ragga, in fact—the one thing it can't be called is Reega; it is Ryega or something toward Ragga from that. (This etymology is pure speculation, of course. Yet the name invites speculation. It seems, for instance, unlike any Indian names in the neighborhood. What can it be then?)

Government maps, incidentally, apply the name Mount Riga only to a small peak at the south edge of the Riga plateau. But this is not the current usage of the region. In Salisbury, "Mount Riga" means at least the Connecticut and New York State parts of the whole eminence, which covers about fifty square miles and is called, officially, the Taconic Range. Often the term takes in the Massachusetts part as well (and one hears the word Raggy applied to the woodsmen of Mount Washington, Mass., a still-alive community).

In my Salisbury boyhood I was enchanted by the idea of the Raggies. The Raggy spirit seemed to me then—as it still does—romantic, independent, and rich in flavor. But I could not have defined what a Raggy was, and I think this is true of many Salisbury people. There is a tendency nowadays to think that anyone who has lived in the township fairly long, and has a reasonably care-free attitude, should be called a Raggy; and from that point the concept moves, through various stages and various minds, to the other limit, the purist one, where Raggies are only those who live the old-time woodsman life on the mountain itself. In this latter sense there have really been no Raggies, in Connecticut at least, for the past half century.

While staying on the mountain last summer, and thinking about it, I concluded that the term made most sense if it were confined to people who had actually lived on Riga or to their descendants still living near by—to families with names like Surdam, Ostrander, Rosseter, and Ball, which are seen on gravestones in the Mount Riga cemetery, or like Bonhotel and Brazee, which, though not found there, are celebrated for a mountain background. There are many with such names still in Salisbury. Often they live on the lower slopes of Mount Riga itself—in the upper edges of the settlements around it—and it is they, by and large, who are still the good woodsmen of our town (or who *were* that—one of them, now in his late fifties, told me last summer that he had walked everywhere on the mountain as a youth, but had years ago been weaned of that habit, or ability, by the automobile).

It is the Raggies, too, who have supplied the town's most vivid folklore. Some of this has been written up, even scurrilously—I have read allegations in print of disreputable, hillbilly Raggy ways; of incest, for instance, and of diets monotonous with woodchuck. Other, less hostile items of folklore are passed on orally in Salisbury. There was, for instance, the man who told his wife one Sunday that he was going to a ball-game in Salisbury village, who did go to it, but who drifted off later to upstate New York, and stayed there for seven years without bothering to write; when he finally came home, after this long absence, his wife looked up from her work and merely asked him what the score of the game had been. There was also the old lady who became chair-bound late in life and who used to pass the months by hatching out eggs, two at a time, in her bosom. Tales like this filled my imagination when I was a boy, and so did the feats of strength and woodcraft attributed to Raggy men. Among the gayest moments of my boyhood were those of attendance at Raggy square-dances, with Raggy callers and fiddlers, and among the nicest people I have known were Raggy men who worked on my father's farm. In my vagueness I didn't identify them strictly then as Raggies, but last summer I pinned them down more closely: at least two former charcoal-burners had come into my life then, and at least two charcoal-burner's sons who had been born on the mountain. To me these men have always seemed admirable, kind, and gentle. Since the age of twelve fate has kept me from Salisbury most of the time—and often from America too—but the ideal of the

Raggies has stayed with me; and my judgment of other peoples, whether Chinese, Tibetans, Greeks, or urban Americans, has always, I think, been colored by it.

Now last summer, on the mountain, I began relating these Raggies of my boyhood to the older plateau history that I was learning about. The process began easily enough when two contemporary Raggies dropped in at my cabin to call. In the course of talking they remarked that the region around me—it was three miles north of Riga Village and three miles south of Mount Washington, Mass.—had also once been inhabited, if sparsely. This was news to me, and so was what they told me next: that a famous search for a little lost Raggy boy, Amos Bonhotel, had taken place in that neighborhood, around the flanks of Bear Mountain. I knew Amos Bonhotel from my childhood, but I hadn't known he had lived on the mountain, nor had I ever heard of his being lost, though I was now told that this had been written up extensively, a year or so ago, in our regional weekly, the *Lakeville Journal*. In time I found this *Journal* story—a series of two articles—and read it. The little Amos, it said indeed, had gone astray on Mount Riga in 1889, while less than three years old—he had been the son of a French collier still living and working there. The mountain population had begun a mass search for him, being joined on the second day by lowland people—more than two hundred, I read, had been on hand by the fourth day, when the boy was found. From the *Journal* I also learned that Amos was still alive and in Salisbury, and I felt he might supply what I was hunting for: a present link with the teeming mountain past. So I looked him up, but I found, alas, that he could tell me little. He had left the mountain while still very small, he said—soon after his escapade—and though living in Salisbury since then had not even been up on it for the past twenty years.

In the end I got more in the way of recall from memories that I luckily had of Amos's brother, Louis Bonhotel, whom I had also known in boyhood and whom I had met by chance a decade earlier—in 1953—during a Salisbury visit. I had been walking then in the mountain's foothills—above Route 41, between Salisbury and Sage's Ravine—and had come, to my surprise, on a nice, well-lived-in little shanty by a stream. Louis Bonhotel had been standing in the cabin's yard, and he had recognized me and asked me in for a glass of wine. It had been cosy inside, with a couple of hound-dogs on the floor and with pots and dishes left around in manly, unsterile abandon. The place had been a hermitage and Louis had seemed imbued with the hermit spirit. I had been wearing an old canvas jacket fastened with safety-pins, and he had looked at them approvingly. "Those are the real bachelor's buttons," he had said. "That's what I use myself." And he had opened his own jacket to show a costume agleam with pins beneath it.

Later I had been told that Louis hunted incessantly on the mountainside—hunted rabbits, squirrels, everything —and also that he raised fine vegetables near his shanty, though he got little good from them as he usually gave them away to friends and acquaintances. The more I thought about Louis, last summer, the more I saw him as the ideal Raggy, preserved into modern times, and the more I wished he was around to furnish the link that Amos couldn't furnish.

But he wasn't around—he had died in 1961, God rest his soul—and I had to look elsewhere. This took time, but eventually, in September, I found two brothers who had been born and bred on Mount Riga—though they seemed innocent of the wilder Raggy ways—and whose family had been the last of the old-timers to leave it. Their names were Harris and Willis Rosseter, they now lived in houses side by side in Salisbury, and they were courteous, soft-spoken men in their seventies. They well remembered Riga Village, which had kept on as a dwindling settlement long after the furnace had shut down— it had kept on till 1908, in fact, the year of the Rosseter's departure.

The Rosseter family had lived on the mountain a long time, the brothers said, perhaps even since 1810. Their own great-grandfather had run a sawmill there, making lumber for the houses in the settlement, and their grandfather had been a puddler at the furnace, helping to make pigs—their father had worked in the woods, I gathered; it was the only paying employment left by his time. Harris Rosseter, the older brother, remembered going to school on the mountain, in the early 'nineties, with thirty other children—Surdams, Ostranders, Balls, Thurstons, and so on. He also remembered seeing charcoal burned up there—it couldn't have been later than 1898, he and Willis figured when they discussed it. That had been the last of the Riga charcoal, which till the end had gone to newer furnaces down on the lowlands; it had been hauled down the mountain, the brothers said, on wagons with high sloping sides like corncribs.

Thereafter the still-resident Raggies, fewer year by year, had continued working in the woods—clearing firetrails or getting out cordwood, mine-timbers, and the like. Even after 1908 Willis Rosseter had worked up there in the good seasons, cutting timbers to support mine passages at Ore Hill. The timbers had been of chestnut and either six or fourteen feet long, depending on their destined use—the fourteen-footers had had to be six inches through at their narrow end. Willis had skidded them part way down the mountain on a path, after which mine teams had hauled them on by wagon. He had cut those mine-timbers till 1910 or 1912. He had had a horse, he remembered, so knowing that it could almost skid the logs by itself.

The brothers reminisced some more about the earlier days. They remembered working in the woods with oxen hitched to wood-shod sleds, and they remembered hitching yokes of oxen behind heavy laden horse-drawn wagons—to hold them back—while going down the mountain. It sounded very primitive to me, as indeed it was.

They went on talking, now one and then the other, answering my questions.

"We had a good farm on the mountain," one of them said. "We raised corn, potatoes, oats, and hay. We had up to twenty head of cows, milking twelve or fourteen of them."

"We carried all our own water," said the other brother, "from a well a hundred feet from the house. We carried it in buckets, and that was hard. Sometimes the well went dry in summer, and then we carried it all the way from the lake. We had good oak firewood, and we must have burned twenty-five cord a year." The brothers shook their heads in wonderment—twenty-five cords would fill a six-car garage.

"We had three fireplaces downstairs in the house," said one brother. "They were of brick, but all three rested on a big stone platform in the basement. The kitchen fireplace was very wide." Between them the brothers demonstrated, measuring off ten or twelve feet on a wall of the room where we were talking. "There was a crane over the fire," said one. "Then there were two kettles hanging to the left of that, also for cooking, and an oven —a bake-oven—built into the righthand side."

"We did all our own baking," said the other brother. "We brought up our flour, from Salisbury, by the barrel, and we brought up our sugar in twenty-five-pound sacks."

"We would butcher a couple of beeves in the fall," said the first brother, "and two or three pigs. We would have corned beef and salt pork right through the winter, and it was good. We would have fifty bushels of potatoes in the cellar, and eight barrels or more of apples—we would have whole bins of apples there. And plenty of cabbage, beets and carrots. We lived very well in that time."

"We would have apples until May," said the other brother, nodding. "You could really keep things in those old dirt cellars."

And that was the plateau life in the good old days. And it ended permanently in 1908.

Some say the Riga furnace shut down in 1847, while others—including those responsible for a plaque now mounted at the site—say it continued till about 1860. Anyway it must have been shut before the Civil War, and besides that the business had evidently stopped booming as early as the eighteen-thirties. Railroads seem to have been the main trouble. As time passed it grew easier for ironmasters to make their iron wherever they wanted—near the good markets, say—by using railways to assemble the raw materials. Had the Riga furnace been more accessible it might have been dealt into a rail net itself, but this was out of the question. Its up-and-down hauling got more and more anachronistic, and the new age passed it by.

Yet Salisbury iron-making as a whole did not cease then—the name Salisbury was often applied to iron produced in a large district roundabout, workable deposits having been found up to fifty miles from Salisbury itself. By the late nineteenth century, according to Miss Pettee, some fifty furnaces were working in the district. They were spotted about in places like East Canaan, Kent, and the Cornwalls in Connecticut; like Dover Furnace, Millerton, Ancram, and Copake in New York; and like Richmond and West Stockbridge in Massachusetts. Today the whole region is a sleepy, peaceful one with little more startling than dairy cows and neat houses to mark the human presence, but a hundred years ago it was comparable to the English Midlands. Charcoal smoked on the hilltops, furnaces belched in the lowlands, and ore, pigs, and limestone went to and fro on the roads and rails. The newer furnaces were more civilized than the Mount Riga one; they were made of well-dressed stone now, often mortared together, and they had real arches —even handsome Gothic ones—over their hearth doors. But their dimensions were about the same as those of Riga and so, essentially, was their mode of operating.

Not all the district's iron was of the best grade. I have heard about one ore-bed for instance, not far from Mount Riga, whose output was sent, humiliatingly, to Pennsylvania for stove-making. But the ore at least from Ore Hill, in Salisbury, and from Richmond, Mass., continued in great demand for gun-making through the Civil War. Extra-high-grade, and extra-expensive, cannon were made in that war by one Horatio Ames in a foundry at Amesville, on the bank of the Housatonic in Salisbury township. He turned out fifty-pounders and then eighty-pounders, the biggest wrought-iron guns made till then in the U.S.—the Union Government even ordered 125-pounders from him toward the war's end. A Captain G. V. Fox, Assistant Secretary of the Navy, later testified that "In my opinion, Mr. Ames has made the best wrought-iron guns in the world." (I have also read, in a newspaper story, that the plates for the *Monitor* were of Salisbury iron, but I haven't verified this from other sources.)

After Mount Riga shut down, the mining and smelting of iron in Salisbury township were controlled by the Barnum Richardson Company, later known as the Salisbury Iron Company. Its headquarters were at Lime Rock, in the town's southeast corner, and it had two foundries there, making various things from its iron, most notably extra-durable wheels for railway cars. The company went out of business in the mid-nineteen-twenties, after which Salisbury iron was finished, but before that time —in the last decades of the nineteenth century and first ones of the twentieth—it prospered mightily. For a while it had eight furnaces going full blast in Salisbury and nearby towns. It also outran the local charcoal supply and began importing, by rail, from the South Atlantic seaboard. This was dangerous because the charcoal was sometimes carelessly loaded while a bit of it was still aglow—then the breezes of travel might fan it into a blaze. I have read one account of a burning charcoal train coming down grade "like a big comet" toward the company's furnaces at East Canaan (luckily this train left the tracks and burned out in a field).

In its last decades the company got ore mainly from its mine at Ore Hill, which became a bigger and bigger operation. Originally an open pit, it had elaborate shaft-work by the end, going down through some four levels. A village developed at Ore Hill, which I remember from my boyhood, though it is nearly all gone now. It had a post-office, a school, a store, and a railway station, together with a residential shantytown on the brow of the mine itself. Recent immigrants, instead of Raggies, lived there and worked the mine—a few Poles and Italians and a great many Irishmen—Saint Patrick's Day was the big event of Ore Hill's year. Many Irish families still live in Salisbury township (though few in Ore Hill itself), and their names are a witness to those mining days.

The names remain, but like everything else in Salisbury they have little ferrous connotation now. The mining is a memory, dimmer year by year, and the mines themselves, at Ore Hill and elsewhere, are mere ponds, in keeping with the newer Salisbury landscape. One often hears the Bessemer process blamed for the end of Salisbury iron. Steel, through the use of that process, can be made cheaply, in great volume, and more or less to fit the customers' specifications. Thus the virtues of superior ore, carefully smelted into iron with good charcoal, have come to be less important than they were—not enough so to justify the now costly handicraft technology involved.

Ironically, the Bessemer process was brought to this country, and much improved here, by a certain Alexander Lyman Holley, a metallurgical genius born in Salisbury township, whose father and grandfather had been leaders in the local iron industry. There are some who, in relating this story, treat Holley as a sort of Oedipus or killer of the goose that laid the golden eggs. Yet if one ponders the matter one can't help thinking that the end was coming anyway. Today iron is mined in vast quantities in the Mesabi Range of Minnesota. It goes great distances, by boat and rail, to centers like Pittsburgh, Gary, and Chicago, where it is smelted in huge furnaces with mountains of Pennsylvania coal. And then it is used, in the thousands of tons, by Detroit and other mass consumers in the Great Lakes region. One feels that everything in this routine, and not just the Bessemer process, is out of scale with dear old Salisbury. Our town was a good early phase of the iron rocket. It helped to launch American industry and helped protect it through its infant days. Now American industry is orbiting in the Middle West, and Salisbury is once more green and quiet.

VI. THE TOWN

A CHANGE I have studied most recently in Salisbury is
in the institution of the town itself, and its significance
(a "town," or township, in our usage is an area compris-
ing one or more villages and their hinterlands; the town
of Salisbury includes the villages of Salisbury, Lakeville,
Amesville, Ore Hill, Lime Rock, and Taconic). My interest in the subject was aroused awhile ago when I noticed that the towns in Connecticut—and also Massachusetts, which is our mother-state—are roughly the same
size. A year ago I was living in Cambridge, Mass., and
bicycling into the country on weekends, and I found the
town centers clicking by quite regularly: Belmont, Lex-
ington, Concord, Acton; or Weston, Lincoln, Concord,
and so on. I felt there must be a reason for this uniform-
ity, and I began looking into it—began asking, also,
what were the original functions of a New England town
and how well they had endured.

I found, of course, that our towns are not wholly uni-
form in size, though they are more so than the nations of
Europe, say, or the fifty states of the U.S. Salisbury itself
is bigger than most other Connecticut towns, according
to the state's official *Register and Manual;* it is tied for
second place in size with its neighbor Sharon—New Mil-

ford, a little to Sharon's south, being the only one that is
bigger. Some of our towns are a good deal smaller, too,
because they have split up by binary fission, which Connecticut law allows if the population of each fragment
is a certain size. There is perhaps no limit on how small
a town can be, if it is densely populated, but there is a
practical limit in the other direction. The Connecticut
towns of Kent and Litchfield were once bigger than they
are now, and also bigger than Salisbury, but they split
up long ago—Kent throwing off Warren and Litchfield,
Morris—presumably because their size was unmanage-
able. So one assumes that towns much bigger than Salisbury, which is roughly nine miles by seven, are not
viable, or were not in the past. (I have also read that
Salisbury men, in the late eighteenth century, founded
three new towns in west-central Vermont, and that each
was six miles square.)

From the writings of Miss Julia Pettee, our local historian, and from speeches made in the mid-nineteenth
century by Judge Samuel Church, another town lumi-
nary, I have further gathered that Salisbury's size was
set mainly by ecclesiastical factors. It is hard nowadays
to realize how theocratic the early Connecticut was. Yet
our settlers, or their forebears, were religious exiles who
had crossed the ocean to practise their faith, of Calvinis-
tic Protestantism. They did this through the Congregational Church, which was official in Connecticut and was
supported by the state's political organs, including the
various towns, until 1818, when it was disestablished.
And so before Salisbury was allowed to incorporate, the
state government, in Hartford, sent a survey party to de-
cide if the area could support a minister (our town is
large, but perhaps half its surface is taken up by non-

arable lakes and mountains). The party's report was fa-
vorable; the town incorporated in 1741; and the next
step was to find the minister himself and establish him
in dignity. A young man named Jonathan Lee finally got
the call; he was made a proprietor of the town—was
given one twenty-fifth of its public lands—and was also
paid a salary; and later, after forty-five years of service
and a good deal of land speculation, he had become a
rich man by the standards of his time.

After choosing a minister, the people had next to build
a meeting-house. Judge Church, in a centennial speech
about Litchfield County, to which Salisbury belongs, said
that "the meeting-house was . . . seen at the central
point of each town, modestly elevated above surrounding
buildings." In Salisbury it was exactly at the center in
theory, though a little apart from this because of faulty
surveying. The original plan was to build it a few hundred yards south of this supposed center, but the parish-
ioners on the north edge of town objected and won out
after a few years of deadlock, in which no building was
done. The placement was important, I have learned from
Miss Pettee and others, because all the citizens were le-
gally bound to attend both a morning and an afternoon
service on Sundays. Failures were punishable by fines;
perhaps these were never actually levied in Salisbury,
but at least there was a pressure to conform. Little Sab-
bath-day houses were built on land near the meeting-
house, and the farther-out families would bring their
lunch to these and sit around fires there between the two
services in winter (the meeting-house itself was not
heated). There were no carriage-roads in the early Salisbury, and men who could afford it would ride in and out
on horseback, with their wives on pillion seats. Others

would have to walk in and out, which is still not easy in
the two ends of a winter day.

One can drive a car across Salisbury now in fifteen
minutes, without going over forty miles an hour. I tested
that last winter, with a friend, and I have also found
more interesting ways to explore the space question. Two
years ago I was living in a cabin in the northwest corner
of town, and I found I could walk from there into the
center in about three hours. Then this past winter I have
experimented with skis. One peculiarity of Salisbury is
that it became a great ski town back in the 1920s, long
before the vogue in this country of downhill—slalom—
skiing. The art was brought here by a Norwegian family of brothers named Satre, who specialized in cross-
country skiing and in jumping, and who inspired many
of our youths to follow their example. I never dared try
jumping, but in my teens I did ski cross-country a good
deal. Then last winter I took it up again, using some old
—Satre vintage—skis and boots belonging to my brother.
I skied mainly on the almost-abandoned tracks of the
Central New England Railroad, where there are no
fences or other obstacles. It was fascinating, apart from
the exploration of space, because Salisbury is so beautiful, and I had not spent a winter here for over a decade.
I learned again about the different qualities of snow—
crunchy snow, sticky snow, and fluffy silent snow, also
snow with a rhinestone sparkle in the sun. The trees were
dark against it, and the brooks were black. I would see
the tracks of animals and of partridge. I would see the
partridge themselves; they seemed to be tamer with the
hunting season closed, and to fly straighter against the
blue sky. I saw four deer once too, crossing a field in
single file, and I would have seen more except that I

always took my brother's black retriever along. He chased the animals away from me, but he was fun himself: a black dog bounding heroically through the deep whiteness.

Often we followed the railway from my brother's house, which is near the town's center, up to Twin Lakes, which is in its northern part. We would see men fishing through the ice there, and would feel the north wind coming down from Massachusetts. And then on Sundays we would go past the lakes and follow the track, which makes a right turn there, clear over to the Housatonic River, which is the town's east boundary. This would take a varying time, depending on the snow. Once I made it to the river and back in four and a half hours, but once again, on a sticky day, it took me almost seven. And on these trips I would think about the remoter of the early townsmen. Their conditions were different—they had snowshoes, or nothing, instead of skis—but it was plain, anyway, that they had a bitter task in winter. Calvinism or no Calvinism, they could hardly have been asked to travel farther.

The town's civil functions were important from the beginning, of course, even if the Church was paramount. Town meetings were held from the time of incorporation: both special meetings, to discuss particular issues, and annual ones where officials were elected. Among those elected at the first town meeting, according to minutes still in existence, were a "Town Clearke"; three selectmen; a constable; three "Surveyours of high ways"; three "Branders of horses"; three "Listers"; one "Pound Keeper"; three "Fence Viewers"; a "Collector"; a "Sealer of Leather"; and a "Town Treasurer Sealer of Weights and Measures." Some of these titles, like the branders, seem wholly archaic today. Branders were needed then because there were few fences, and animals roamed at large. They could be identified inside the town without branding, but if they strayed outside they couldn't. So the different towns had their different brands, Salisbury's being like a Greek cross. The whole problem of grazing—of whether pigs, for instance, should be "admitted as commoners," i.e. allowed on public land—took up much time in the early meetings. Horses, hogs, cattle, and ewes were generally admitted as commoners; rams were ruled out in 1746.

Other town business in those early days included the payment of bounties on wolves (now long gone from Salisbury) and on rattlesnakes, crows, and squirrels (now still around). Of course roads were important, and road-building was a main activity. There was also the maintenance of law and order, and the town had authority to keep unruly people out. The neighborhood had a brander before incorporation in 1741, but otherwise these very local matters, if dealt with at all, had to be referred tediously to Hartford, which was another reason for creating the town. After it was created the selectmen ran the machinery with help from the other officials, and the town clerk kept the public records and those of births, marriages, deaths, and land transfers. (The clerk's job was part-time then and held by a man; now it is full-time and held by a woman, Lila Nash.)

Education was prominent from the beginning, the teacher being second only to the minister in importance. He taught the three Rs, at three settlements in the town, residing in each for three or four months of the year; log cabins were put up there to house his work. There was no official secondary schooling, but the minister taught some boys, at least, in private at his home (afterward they might go to Yale, days of travel away, which was strictly Congregational then).

A gristmill and a sawmill were thought necessary to each town in the region, and some town governments encouraged them. Salisbury's didn't have to; with good water-power and enterprising inhabitants, the town had *two* gristmills and *two* sawmills even in the early days. She also had at least one blacksmith shop, making useful things from local iron. Her commerce with the outside world—which was small, because even cloth and clothing were home-made—seems largely to have been handled by peddlers. They often came from the Hudson River, instead of some Connecticut center, because of another Salisbury peculiarity: the presence of the Housatonic all down its eastern side. The Housatonic, a good-sized stream, was not bridged in the early eighteenth century, but had to be swum, crossed in a canoe or forded, the last being possible at only one or two points. Therefore the Hudson Valley, only twenty miles away and well developed by that time, had a commercial advantage.

Most of these facts I have got from reading Miss Pettee and Judge Church. I have also got from them a vivid impression of the town's nature: it was a primitive, well-knit community, hewing a living from the forest; working hard and gathering together each Sunday, an occasion whose meaning was as much social, perhaps, as religious; running its secular affairs through the town meeting and the selectmen and other officers, a good example of the legislative and executive in a simple democracy (the town also got a justice of the peace in

1745). It was a functioning module, scaled to the speed of travel and unified by the interweaving of its people's lives.

It was not sovereign; it derived all its powers, as it still does, from the statutes of the Connecticut General Assembly. Yet it had its share in writing those statutes. Its people voted as individuals for the governor and for a senator in the Assembly's upper house, and the town itself sent two representatives to the lower, as the states later sent them to the U.S. Senate (in Salisbury's case this didn't actually begin till 1757, because the town didn't pay taxes to Hartford before that). While not sovereign, the town was self-reliant and had a strong sense of identity. In most things it ran its own business, in a hard-headed Yankee way, and in state affairs it represented a local view.

I read about all this, and imagined it, as the winter passed. Then with the coming of March two things occurred: spring also came, with a rush, and I began looking into modern Salisbury. The coming of spring was unusually definite. On the last day of February I skied up to the lakes and felt the cold north wind again. I saw the riffled expanse of snowy ice, with the fishermen on it, and I saw the animal tracks, and the blobs of snow on the old nests in the thickets. The days were longer than they had been, I noted as I came home, yet the winter was still with us. Then on March 1 the winds began coming from the south, and were changeable; the snow began really thawing then, under a warm sun, and it was very sticky. The next day there were patches of bare ground on the track, and no skiing there, though the woods still had deep corn-snow in them. I tried that, and it was passable, but heavy going. Then on March 3 and 4 the corn-snow kept on melting, and got heavier still, and I gave up skiing altogether. I took to walking on the track, which was almost bare now. On March 5 I rose and saw a south wind, a roaring one, blowing white mists off the remaining snow patches. That kept up all day, with the mists like steam, and the patches shrank. The brooks were in wild spate by then—were a gray-brown color, with a dark light above them—and there was a warm, oppressive feeling in the air. On March 7 I saw a redwing blackbird, the first returning migrant, and on the eighth my dog put up fifteen or twenty mallards in a big old cornfield by a brook; the field was bare, but wet, and the ducks flew tamely over it, quacking. I saw a woodcock that day too, flying off with its long bill and whistling wings, and my nephew saw a northbound V of geese.

As for modern Salisbury, I began asking officials and other friends about it, and I learned, as I had expected, that our independence has diminished in many, though not all, ways. (I learned too that Salisbury is a less reliable microcosm than I had thought, or at least is not very typical of the towns around it, but that is something to take up later.) The town's loss of power is obscured by a growth in the officialdom, which now boasts almost a hundred full- or part-time functionaries (some four times as many as in the beginning) and which includes all kinds of offices and organs, like a town social worker, a food inspector, a recreation commission, and a planning and zoning commission, that were undreamt of by the founding fathers. The work of this structure is coordinated, too, by a first selectman of increased importance, a virtual full-time mayor. But these additions arise

from the complexities of modern life—the new ideas of
what government should do for people—rather than
from growth in the town's own power. They are offset
partly by the loss of branders, fence viewers, and sealers
of leather, but still more by state and federal encroach-
ments in road-building, law-enforcement, and other old
town activities.

Salisbury in the beginning was so primitive that one
can hardly take it as a yardstick for comparison with the
modern town. One can better take the whole development through the eighteenth, nineteenth, and early
twentieth centuries. One can often find a curve of town
functions passing through this time: first the function is
non-existent or rudimentary; then it appears and grows
or proliferates as the town gets richer and more sophisti-
cated; then it contracts, or disappears off the town map
altogether, as modern communications speed up.

Welfare is an example. At first Salisbury had no poor,
according to Miss Pettee, and made no provision for
them, but after a few decades the town took up the cus-
tom, then standard in Connecticut, of farming out the
care of paupers to the lowest bidder. This made for care
of the worst possible kind; it came to prick the people's
conscience; and in 1829 a Salisbury Asylum was established, in a former inn, with quarters for the indigent
plus a "bettering place" for wrongdoers, under heavy
lock and key, on the second floor. This was wholly a town
enterprise, paid for by town funds. The place became too
large as the nineteenth century went on—as charities
and other social services arose to share the load—and it
was abandoned for a smaller building. Yet the institution, of a town poor-farm, continued; there was still a
poor-farm in my boyhood, in the 1920s. Today it is gone,

though, supplanted by the Welfare State. Town poor who need hospital care are sent elsewhere, and relief money disbursed in the town is supplied by the Connecticut government, though its distribution is still supervised by our first selectman. The state believes, that is, that local people still know the needs best, but it holds that the money must be raised by taxes on a larger scale.

The town's school system has also followed the curve. In the beginning we had no high school, as already noted; in my boyhood we did have one—I suppose it began in the nineteenth century; but now the work has been taken over by a broader institution, the Housatonic Valley Regional High School, which lies just outside our border and serves six towns of northwest Connecticut. For us it is a real improvement, given modern transport; all the Salisbury students live within ten miles of the new school, and they get better and more varied teaching than they did—the old town high school had 119 students at the end, whereas the H.V.R.H.S. now has 671; it has a faculty of forty-two and various facilities, like a federally supported "vocational agricultural center," that could hardly have been swung on a town basis.

The H.V.R.H.S. was the first regional high school in New England, but now there are many others, and one gathers that a new module, bigger than the town, is trying to shape up. With us the module holds for a number of things besides just education; it goes part way toward having the early town's community functions. The H.V. R.H.S. has the biggest auditorium in our region, and that draws people together. So do the sports at its playing fields. And then there is romance. Many boys and girls at the high school start going together in their freshman year, or a bit later, and they keep it up, through graduation, till in the end they marry: Cornwall boys marry Salisbury girls and so on. They settle in each other's towns and homogenize us.

Then again our weekly, the *Lakeville Journal*, was strictly a town paper in my boyhood, but it went regional in the high school's wake. Its publisher, Stewart Hoskins, says that he expected the high school to break down the town barriers, and that it did so; the *Journal* is now putting out the same editorial fare to all six towns (plus a seventh, Norfolk, that has come its way by chance). The paper's circulation, staff, and plant have increased about tenfold in going regional, Hoskins adds. "Everything is ten times as big," he says, "including the expenses."

Nor is that all. There are certain cultural societies here, like the Housatonic Music Association and a forum called Opinions Unlimited, that also follow the high-school region. In my boyhood such things, if they existed at all, would probably have been on the town scale. But now people cross the lines to go to them. They cross the lines for social mixing, too, much more than they did. (Churchgoing, oddly, continues pretty much on the town scale with us. Our churchgoing is now in several denominations, of course, and it is a conservative affair. Our parishes may well have more survival value than the town itself.)

To get back to education, primary schooling has followed the curve I have described. The early Salisbury had one rotating school-teacher, but by 1766, according to Miss Pettee, there were nine school districts in town and 480 pupils. By the late nineteenth century we had thirteen districts, each with a schoolhouse to which the pupils in that part of town could walk. About half of these buildings were abandoned by the 1930s, and as a small boy I remember the ruins of our own district school, the one nearest my family's farm; I remember a pile of debris near the road, with bits of smashed yellow-wood desks and black cast-iron fittings. By then, thanks to the automobile, the grade pupils were being concentrated, and the process has continued until now they are all in one central school, a modern plant finished in 1953. It has two or three teachers for each grade plus special ones in French, art, music, and so on. It has so far refrained from going regional; a few years ago a movement was launched here for regional junior high schools, including the seventh and eighth grades, but Salisbury voted against it. Our primary school is now the most expensive item in our town budget, and some here say it is the chief town function still remaining. Even so it gets much supervision, plus a fifth or a quarter of its income, from the state; and the fact that it feeds into the regional high school tends to level it off with schools in the surrounding towns, where—for reasons we shall soon go into—there is often less interest in education and less money available to pay for it. So even in this intimate matter we are not an island now.

We needn't labor through all the town's executive functions (its main legislative function, the town meeting, can be touched on later). With one notable exception the story is the same with all our enterprises: more personnel involved nowadays, more plant and equipment, more expenditure, and less autonomy.

The one exception is the field of zoning, where the town recently acquired, and apparently intends to use, great new powers for preserving its character and resisting change. Salisbury's nature and its economic history

are special. The town began like the neighboring ones, as
a community of virtually self-sufficient homesteaders,
but it was soon distinguished by the presence of iron
within its borders.* Iron boomed especially in the Revolution, the War of 1812, the Civil War, and the industrial expansion that followed. Our town was a smoky,
grimy hive of activity during much of that time. Then
the activity collapsed around the turn of the century
when iron came to be worked, with the new technology,
on a far bigger scale in the Middle West. Our population
fell from 3715 in 1880 to 2497 in 1920, and no doubt
more would have left us if they could have found a living
elsewhere. Many of the survivors got by on dairy-farm-
ing, for which our terrain was then well suited and for
which the railroads were opening up ever better markets
in New York (100 miles distant) and other cities. But
dairying was a less intense use of the land than iron-
working, and the population might have dwindled further if another source of income had not arisen, in a resort and boarding-school trade exploiting our lakes and
mountains (at least one writer, early in this century,
called us another Switzerland). Three boarding schools
—Hotchkiss, Salisbury, and Indian Mountain—were established here in the decades when iron was failing. Ho-
tels sprang up then too, but soon they became less important than the purchase, or renting, of houses and
farms by summer people or year-round retired people.
My grandmother, a widow with some children and a
little money, came to Salisbury just after 1900 and
bought a farm. I think she was something of a pioneer—
I think nearly all her neighbors had proper economic
and historical roots in the town—but her example was

* See Chapter V.

followed more and more as time passed. In the 'twenties and 'thirties many families came here because they liked it and could afford it, and a real flood has come since VJ-Day. Those of modest means have bought small houses, and those of larger have bought old farms and remodeled them—perhaps taking them out of production too, for the dairy business is on the wane here. The continuity of ownership in town has been affected by the influx. In the old days, when our farms were really farms, they would pass from generation to generation in the same families, but now that they are estates they seldom do. Unless a family is very rich its sons or sons-in-law can't afford to maintain a big place so far from the centers of employment; they must disperse and live, with their own young families, in the cities or true suburbs. And so when an elderly couple dies here now, their place is apt to be sold. Continuity of ownership is lost, but continuity of character, surprisingly, is not, for another very similar family usually buys the place, at whatever price, with the same end in view: to live quietly in our rural landscape. Thus iron, and to some extent cows, have ceased to be an issue with us; as long as Wall Street puts out coupons we are in business.

Meanwhile, of course, urban sprawl has been moving toward us from the coastal megalopolis. It has made inroads especially on Canaan and Millerton, the town centers to our east and west. Both these points have been served, since the mid-nineteenth century, by good railroads from New York, and partly as a result their character is different from ours. Their main streets are gritty and commercial; their populations contain big elements of the more recent immigrant stocks; they are largely Catholic, with a high birth rate; and they look on the coming of industry, or virtually any other change, as a good thing. Salisbury for its part is more conservative. It is still Anglo-Saxon Protestant in the main. It has a low birth rate, partly because its people believe in birth control and partly because they are, on the average, getting old. Our town is rich—"one of the wealthiest small communities in the U.S.A.," a lawyer here told me the other day. Some of the richer townsmen have never fought economic battles; others have fought them elsewhere; and few but the less privileged now look on Salisbury as terrain for that kind of thing. The rest look on it as a place for quietude, amid the woods and fields.

And our planning and zoning commission, if I rightly understand its chairman, Gordon Reid, and its secretary, Martha Atchley, will see to this. The commission was established after much controversy, expressed in stormy town meetings in the 'forties and 'fifties, and—like other zoning commissions in the Connecticut towns that choose to have them—was given huge powers under state law, provided only that it should work out a master plan, with attendant regulations, and hold hearings where the public might criticize it all. Those things have been done now, and a policy, to keep Salisbury much as is, has been evolved. One may not bring a trailer to Salisbury now and live in it. One may not subdivide real estate without observing elaborate rules. And while one may build a factory here in theory, one must so beautify it, decontaminate it, and satisfy the neighbors about its gentility, that anything like dark Satanic mills can no longer get a foothold with us. This is different from the situation in the 'twenties and 'thirties, when a man could set up a billboard or factory almost at will. We have struck a blow against the oppressions of economic law. At first one deems this a gallant rearguard action, against centrality, by a strong and independent fragment of New England. But then one wonders. The stand does show local strength of a sort, but not strength really based on Salisbury. The early settlers, and the iron miners and dairy farmers who followed them, had autonomy because their sustenance came from the soil here. Most of our modern residents, on the other hand, get their sustenance, directly or indirectly, from distant sectors of the great U.S. economy—sectors that are hard to understand from here, in their workings, but that keep paying off and making us all reasonably prosperous, whether we are the coupon-cutters themselves or the teachers, tradesmen, and artisans who serve the coupon-cutters. While staving off the megalopolis, our community has, in fact, become a specialized part of it: a sanctuary for those megalopolitans who needn't embrace the grime and clatter themselves. And thanks to zoning we may stay that way. Canaan and Millerton may well industrialize—the process is going on apace in them—and meanwhile we, growing more and more special, may keep our scenery unspoiled. The prospect is delightful, but still one cannot equate the present Salisbury with the old self-reliant one.

March continued, and—while learning these facts and thinking about them—I went on enjoying our now-protected landscape. I walked almost wholly on the railroad, for the woods, what with mud and remaining snow patches, were still hard going. Our railroad is a vestige of the late nineteenth century, the boom-time of railwaying in the nation and of iron in our town. It used to be a grand affair, helping to link Boston with the West, and up into my boyhood it still carried passengers. I have ridden on it as a passenger, indeed, and once I even rode in the cab with the engineer. But the passenger trade ceased in 1927, and since then the road's freight traffic, and the length of the line itself, have dwindled. Now only eight or nine miles of track are left, and over this a train moves haltingly once or twice a week, bearing things like fuel oil and building materials into Salisbury from Canaan.* The trains are informal and obliging— stopping even to let dogs get out of their way—and the ties are scant hindrance to a walker, for little mainte- nance is done on them. Often they have rotted, and in some stretches they have vanished wholly beneath the ground. In my March walking I could see this process at work. The frost was coming out then, and in places I would see new mud-heaves between the ties, standing an inch or two above them—ready to settle down again and help in covering them. The road, I felt, was much like the rest of Salisbury: a once harsh and vital thing, economically, now turning quiet and enjoyable.

In March too I began seeing pussy-willows in the swamps beside the track, though otherwise the scene, ex- cept for the steady vanishing of snow, was little changed. The swamps still had their tall evergreens. The moun- tains had their red-brown cover, of leafless trees, with streaks of birch among it. But the fields were in brown grass now, with here and there a mouse-run exposed by the snow's departure. Also the birds were getting thicker; the swamps were filling up with redwings, and soon the robins and many others were on hand. In February I had

* As of 1967, the track has been entirely ripped up.

heard little but chickadees, or the hammering of wood-peckers, or—toward dusk—the hooting of an owl. But now in March I heard all kinds of song.

Also in March I got a lucky break in these researches, for two town meetings happened to be held then, a week apart (normally our town has but three or four meetings a year now, with months going by between them). There is a *mystique* about New England towns—partly obscuring, I now feel, their true situation—and this focuses on the town meeting, so often hailed as a sample of pure democracy (not to mention a cradle of liberty and a school of politics for the young). I had already been discussing town meetings with a few local friends and had found some pessimism about their tendencies, along with an agreement that their scale, at least, was still right—that they brought together a group of people who knew each other and could co-operate. "Essentially the town meeting is a good instrument of government," one friend told me, "but you must have the right attendance. Only on the big emotional issues do we get much of a turnout here now. Otherwise only a few town officers come, along with a few town workmen, a few extra-dutiful citizens, a few people hoping for excitement, and a couple of journalists. That isn't enough to get the town's real sentiment." Another friend said there had been too *much* attendance at some emotion-charged meetings of recent years, especially a couple that had debated zoning. "The crowds at those meetings overflowed the meeting-hall," my friend said, "and had to be kept in touch by a public-addres system. It was a chaos. Nobody knew what was happening." A third friend, a conservative and Republican, complained about the *quality* of our town meetings. "The quality has gone down all the time," he said. "I can

remember when voters here discussed expenditures carefully, after lots of thought, but now they are apt to vote
for almost anything, out of sentimentality. Property
owners complain sometimes about our tax rate, and I
tell them it would be lower if they themselves would attend town meetings and vote to keep expenses down. But
they won't do it. The old town meetings were dominated
by men who knew town business and knew the value of
a dollar, but such men are getting scarce here now."

(Since that conversation I have looked up some figures
and found that our tax rate is relatively low, in fact; it
is the third lowest among thirty-five Connecticut towns
in our size-classification, of 2500 to 5000 population. I
have also found that the attendance is indeed poor at our
town meetings; it rarely approaches a hundred, though
we now have 2155 registered voters, our population having climbed back, by 1960, to 3309—a gain of 800 in
four decades.)

The turnout at my first town meeting in March happened to be quite good: some 96 people, which Lila Nash,
the town clerk, later said was the highest figure in more
than two years. This meeting was called on an important
local issue: Whether to spend about eighty thousand
dollars in renovating our town hall, an old, white, col-
onnaded, colonial-and-federal building—incorporating
part of the original Church meeting-house—of which
our citizens are very proud; it looms large in Salisbury
center and helps give the village an authentic, even post-
card, New England look. For some years, I gathered at
the meeting, insurance companies had complained about
the structure's hand-hewn beams and underpinnings—
said to have been cut partly through when modern
plumbing was installed—and for a year or more the

town officers had been campaigning for an overhaul of its insides that would leave its treasured outer shell intact. They had been criticized by some townsmen, who felt that what they really wanted was lush bureaucratic offices for themselves, but they had gradually overcome this opposition—laying the groundwork at a town meeting in the year previous—and the current session was intended to clinch the decision.

The meeting was scheduled for eight P.M. (the customary hour), and well before that the scene, a long downstairs chamber in the town-hall building, was filling up with citizens. Plans and charts explaining the renovation were already on the walls as they assembled, and others were being put on by Nort Miner, our local architect. Soon the seats began running short, and extra benches were carried in by Bill Barnett, our first selectman, and Ray Silvernail, our town-hall janitor. Then the meeting was called to order, and Robinson Leech, the chairman of our Republican town committee, was elected moderator. First three minor questions on the agenda were dealt with, and then the renovation issue came up. Tom Wagner, our town counsel, arose and read a motion that the money for the work be appropriated. Then George Milmine, chairman of our town finance committee—which has effective veto power in these cases—arose and said that the alterations were desirable, and he next called on Bill Ford, another finance-committee member (and also our judge of probate), to give further explanations. Ford read a state law that allows towns to spread unusual expenses over as much as five years, and said that Salisbury meant to spread this one over three, which would mean adding 1.1 mill to the tax rate (then 23.7 mills) for that period. He took note of some objections to the building costs (which apparently were higher than the local standard), but said these were made necessary by state and federal minimum-wage laws. He also mentioned two neighboring towns that had recently built brand-new town halls, and said that Salisbury (at less expense) could do better than they: could create an "efficient municipal center" while saving a beloved antiquity. And he went into details of the structure itself and what could be done about it. Later there were questions from the floor, and it came out (as news to me at least) that federal money is available to help towns in cases like this, but that Salisbury, in an earlier town meeting, had voted overwhelmingly against applying for it. Now some urged a reconsideration, on the grounds that the earlier meeting had been ill-attended, but Messrs. Barnett, Ford, and others argued, successfully, that perhaps half of any federal money would be wasted in attendant red tape and delays; also that the town's earlier stand had gained nationwide publicity and could not gracefully be abandoned. The town leadership was, in fact, well prepared on the whole issue—having spent a year in conditioning public opinion to it—and the motion to renovate was soon put to a vote and carried, unanimously.

After that the floor was thrown open for other matters, and one citizen arose to ask what the town planned to do about gypsy moths, which were infesting the woods near his house. Moderator Leech called for an answer from first selectman Barnett, who rose and gave a long explanation, quoting Rachel Carson and others, of why he was using restraint in spraying. This seemed to satisfy all present, and Mr. Leech, after congratulating Mr. Barnett on his mastery of the subject, adjourned the meeting, saying only that he felt cheated because it had not been televised. He had just been in New Hampshire, he said, where the primary campaign involving Lodge, Rockefeller, and Goldwater was then raging; he had seen two New Hampshire town meetings on TV; and he implied that Connecticut ones were every bit as interesting. And after that we all went home, I for one feeling that real town business had been done in proper style.

My second meeting was called on an issue involving the town's own power. Originally, as noted above, each Connecticut town held two seats in the lower house of the legislature, and with some exceptions this rule has endured to the present—it is, in fact, written into the state constitution. Meanwhile, of course, many Connecticut towns have given way to cities, but the basic principle, of two seats per town, has remained in force—in recent years one-tenth of all Connecticut voters (they being in the smaller towns) have elected more than half of the lower house's members. This set-up, not surprisingly, has long been attacked by reformist elements in our state, who have called it a rotten-borough system, and it has been correspondingly defended by our more conservative elements, who often feel that country or village people make a sounder electorate than do the city masses. Party factionalism has come strongly into the matter as well, for country people in Connecticut are Republicans, for the most part, and city people Democrats. So there has been controversy, though the situation has seemed unlikely to change through amendment to our constitution, for the lower house's own consent would be needed for this. Recently, however, the U.S. has had a wave of orders from the federal courts, including the Supreme

Court, directing certain states to reform their electoral districting—for the election not only of their U.S. congressmen, but also of their own state legislators. This wave hit Connecticut on February 10, 1964, through a decision of three federal judges sitting as a panel to consider the question. Among other things the judges found, by a two-to-one majority, that our lower house was being wrongly elected and should be redistricted on a one-man-one-vote basis; and they asked the Republican and Democratic parties to suggest ways of doing this. The Democrats set right out to comply, but the Republicans appealed the decision to the Supreme Court. Meanwhile new controversy over the question sprang up everywhere —in the press, in public gatherings, and so on—and as part of this a meeting of small-town leaders, attended by many Democrats but dominated by the Republican, conservative element, was held in Hartford on March 6. This meeting decided to hire lawyers and intervene in the proceedings on behalf of the towns; and it asked the towns themselves to show their support by contributing up to a hundred dollars each toward the effort. It was to consider this request, for funds, that my second town meeting was called, in answer to a citizens' petition.

This meeting was less well attended than my earlier one—perhaps thirty people came—but it was lively, and for me it brought out another aspect of change in the town's significance. Of course the judges' decision itself was a blow to the status of small Connecticut towns—it would, if upheld, give Salisbury something like one-seventh of a seat in the lower house instead of the two we then enjoyed*—but quite apart from that the meet-

* The decision *was* upheld eventually, and Salisbury now does have only one-seventh of a seat in the lower house.

ing's behavior showed that the two-party system, as such, had greatly invaded the town's outlook and helped to sap its independence. In early times party factionalism had been almost absent from our town politics, but by 1841 it had become prominent enough for Judge Church to describe it, in a Salisbury centennial address, as "demoralizing," "disturbing," and "agitating." "I cannot discharge a duty which I owe to the young men of my native place . . . ," the Judge had said, "without entreating them to divest themselves of party and political prejudices." When I had first read these words they had meant little to me, but since that evening's meeting they have come to mean a lot; I feel the Judge had spotted a major trend.

That evening George Milmine, our finance-committee chairman, was elected moderator. He urged those present to avoid political (i.e. party) overtones in the discussion —to speak from the viewpoint of the town—and in fact some speakers did pay lip-service to this principle, but in their actual arguments the Republican speakers talked throughout like Republicans, and the Democrats like Democrats. The Democratic party here—traditionally a minority—has been growing of late, thanks partly to the addition of artists, writers, and other megalopolitan eggheads who have moved in to enjoy our peace and quiet. These newcomers, understandably, are interested in the larger state and national issues, and they help to give their party a more abstract, if fervent, ideological bent here than it seems to have in the Deep South, say, or the teeming cities. There is also a pressure for conformity among our Democrats, and this was evident tonight. All their speakers supported their party line—in favor of redistricting—though they did it in different ways. John

Wedda, our third selectman (a post that always goes to a Democrat), spoke about rotten boroughs in England, and especially about Old Sarum, Salisbury's namesake, which he said had wound up in the end with no inhabitants at all, but with two seats in Parliament. He implied, of course, that this was no way to run a democracy. Spalding McCabe, recently chairman of our Democratic town committee, spoke more than once, bringing out that the town would not be giving its own instructions to the lawyer it might help in hiring, and questioning the wisdom of this procedure. And so on, all to the same end. Some of our longer-resident Democrats, to my certain knowledge, adore Salisbury and have a great *mystique* about it, but their loyalty to its narrow interests was as nothing now, when compared to their zeal for party and for larger principles worked out elsewhere.

The Republican speakers' motivation was harder to assess, if only because the town's narrow interests coincided with their own wish to go on dominating the lower house (our upper house is now dominated by the Democrats, who have also, of late, been electing our governor). A Republican at this town meeting could theoretically have been moved by various feelings: party spirit, say, or dislike of change or of city people, or even just dislike of taxes, which would almost certainly rise with redistricting and urban control. No observer could be sure how these motives were mixed in any Republican that evening, but all the Republican speakers, anyway, stuck to their party line, just like the Democrats—though, also just like the Democrats, they used different arguments. Bill Barnett talked about the town's identity, about checks and balances, and about how well Connecticut was being run as was. Robbo Leech talked about the small-town meeting in Hartford, which he had been to. Tom Wagner defended, from a legal view, the proposed intervention. And so on, again all to the same end. It was not a very real debate, but it was interesting. The arguments on both sides, however specious, were able and were fun to listen to, and they went on for an hour. Then the clock on the Scoville Memorial Library, across the way, struck nine, and soon after that a vote was held, by show of hands. Party again prevailed, and I dare say Judge Church was spinning in his grave; the vote, fourteen to eleven, was rigidly factional, with the Republican side on top.

After that meeting we went home once more, I now thinking that the town did not amount to much, as an entity, where these larger issues were concerned. It had lost its people's affections to the parties, I felt, and this was in line with other trends in the town I had been noticing. It had lost much of its administrative power, after all, to the Welfare State. It had lost much identity to the regional module. It had lost economic independence to the megalopolis, and it might soon be losing legislative power to the cities. All it was really holding onto, I felt, was freedom to do its own housekeeping—to renovate its town hall as it wished, for instance, and especially to preserve its landscape.

But that landscape anyway, to say it again, was a beauty; and day after day, as March ran out, I kept enjoying it with all my senses. It was a blustery time in late March, with trees often bending in the wind, but also with more and more life coming onto the scene. Late in the month the peepers began, in a swamp near my brother's house. I would hear them at night; and some geese moved in then too, and I would hear them honking near my window in the mornings. I saw some dark-headed, white-sided ducks—blue-bills, golden-eyes?—on the Housatonic one Sunday; they were a kind not found, so far as I know, on our smaller streams. And our stiller waters, too, were opening up by then—ice going from the swamps. One day our dog was caught, mildly, in a muskrat trap in swamp water; he stood there patiently while I took it off his foot. Another day he found a duck in a trap himself, and we brought it home and tried to revive it, unsuccessfully. And so the days passed, and soon came Easter; it was early that year. And nature got ready for the greenery and the summer's work.

VII. THE LAKE FISH

THE LAKE-FISH LIFE in Salisbury has changed more radically, perhaps, than any other aspect of the community since I grew up here. These lake-fish changes are less evident than the dry-land ones, especially for someone who no longer fishes, as I have not done since the 1940s. They must be studied indirectly, through talks with fishermen and with the expert biologists whose appearance on the scene has been basic to the changes themselves. The approach through the biologists makes the fish world seem remoter, but it also puts more precision—less of wild rumor and folklore—into our notions about it.

Salisbury town has six lakes of respectable size, apart from innumerable ponds, and they are of three different types. Upper and Lower Riga Lakes, on the plateau in the town's northwest corner, are smallish, rockbound mountain affairs. Long Pond (also called Wononpakook) and West Twin Lake are shallow, mudbound, warm, and weedy. Finally Lakeville Lake (or Wononscopomuc) and East Twin Lake are deeper and larger than the others and, in their lower levels, a good deal cooler; East Twin is the "largest body of water in the state that is suitable for trout and open to public fishing," according to the Connecticut State Board of Fisheries and Game.

These three different types, though I didn't realize it till recently, can support—are almost destined to support—quite different fish populations.

Of the six, Upper Riga Lake was the one I knew best as a boy, not because it was the nearest to my home—it was the farthest—but because some friends of my parents, Judge and Mrs. Warner, had a big rambling camp on its shore and were very hospitable about asking us to stay there or to come and use their boats. Mount Riga was a remote place then, even from Salisbury village at its base. The plateau was a wild woodland, in which the two lakes nestled with camps dotted sparsely and unobtrusively round their edges. When my life began, in 1912, these camps were reached only by foot or by horse-drawn vehicle. During my boyhood, in the 'twenties, autos were used more and more, but I still have vivid memories of climbing the mountain by sleigh in winter, with big parties, to go fishing through the ice. This remoteness gave Mount Riga a fascination that I have since found only in such places as the Tibetan Plateau and the high Andes, and to it was added a tumultuous curiosity I felt then about underwater life. This curiosity left me in later youth—or at least the thrill of it did—but as a boy I churned violently inside at the prospect of swimming anywhere. The prospect of going on Mount Riga and swimming, fishing, or boating in the upper lake was almost unbearably exciting.

The fish population of Upper Riga Lake seemed ideal to me then, inevitably—it was the "given," the best I knew of—and I think it did come close to fulfilling the water's possibilities. At least it was much better than the present population; the quality of Riga fishing has gone down steadily since the 'twenties or 'thirties, for reasons that I have been learning about from the biologists and shall go into presently. In the 'twenties and 'thirties the catchable Riga fish included chain pickerel, small-mouth bass, yellow perch, sunfish, and bullheads. As small boys —fishing with worms or live bait, often off the rocks along the shore—my brothers and I caught vast numbers of perch and sunfish, nearly always little (though once my brother Bill, for a change, caught an eighteen-inch pickerel off a rock). We did such fishing by day; and by night we sometimes went bullheading, sitting in a boat by lamplight, letting our worms down deep to some muddy bottom-patch, and repeatedly pulling in the heavy, struggling fish, which might be up to a foot long. The bullheads were dark and smooth, and they gleamed as they flopped in the light beams. They had spines that pricked our hands, and they had teeth, in their wide whiskery mouths, that pricked our fingers too, for they swallowed a hook deep, and much probing was needed to get it out again. But bullheads made delicious eating the next day, when skinned and deep-fat fried.

That is how we boys fished, and meanwhile the men went after bigger, more dramatic quarry. Judge Warner himself fished for hours a day in the summer, together with a friend named Dave Jones, a Riga mountaineer or "Raggy" who looked after the camp. Judge Warner had a white beard, Dave Jones had gray walrus moustaches, and both men were gaunt and weathered and seemed infinitely old and patient. They would go out to the deepish middle part of the lake and troll there interminably, one rowing slowly along while the other trailed a line with some mysterious combination, as I remember it, of spoons or spinners and live bait. Or they would skitter out there, with a perch belly: they would cut the white belly-skin, with the orange breast-fins, from a smallish perch; would attach this to a hook on a line from a long bamboo pole; and would then twitch it artfully on the lake's surface. They would often raise, and catch, very big pickerel in this way. I am sure they did other arcane things too, but I didn't see much of these. What I saw most often was their return to the camp, say at mid-day, with their remarkable catch. Their boat had a "well" under the oarsman's seat amidships: a watertight compartment fed through a screened-over hole in the bottom. The well would contain a few inches of fresh water, and in this would be lying, say, a couple of twenty-inch pickerel, a twelve-inch bass or two, and a few nine- or ten-inch perch, much bigger than we boys had been catching. The fish would hang there, breathing and moving their fins, and we would marvel at them. And, looking back, I think those catches must have been close to the optimum for that lake. I think the lake had a good "balance" then, and I am sure Judge Warner and Dave Jones were expert fishermen. Nowadays fishermen become expert with the help of elaborate tackle and a wealth of reading matter, in books and magazines. Judge Warner and Dave Jones had few such aids; they had learned by experience, thought, and the teaching of still older men; but I can't believe they were less adept, in any way, than their modern counterparts.

After being admired in the well the fish would be taken out, killed, cleaned, scaled, and passed along to the kitchen, where Mrs. Warner and her daughters might put them in a chowder. Chowders, served from a tureen at a long table on a porch overlooking the lake, were common fare at the camp; and also common were blue-berries picked, often by boat, from bushes around the lake's edge or on its islands. The Warners' cuisine emphasized mountain-grown food—as well as durable food, like hard-tack and potatoes—for the lake really *was* remote then. When the family went up for the summer they stayed up, some member coming down once a week, perhaps, on a shopping trip. The camp had an ice-house, filled each winter from the lake, where perishables could be kept if necessary; but the day of packaged foods was not in sight.

Now, of course, things are different. People still summer in camps by the lake, but they whiz endlessly up and down the mountain in their cars; one meets such campers any time in the Salisbury Market, at the mountain's base, where they have come to buy their frozen dinners. They depend not a whit on the lake fish now, and in step with this development the fish themselves have shrunk to sizes that make them hardly worth eating. In the summer of 1955 a certain F. J. Trembley, a graduate student in aquatic biology, made a survey of both Upper and Lower Riga Lakes for their owners (descendants of the Warners and of two or three other families who had bought the plateau up, together, early in this century). Trembley did a lot of gill- and trap-netting, which are ways of catching fish for counting and eventual return to the water. In the upper lake he found no traces of the small-mouth bass that had been common a few decades earlier, which indicates that they may be extinct there. He found a huge population of bullheads, but they were all small, between five and seven-and-a-half inches long—"severely stunted and quite worthless," in his words. He did net some big pickerel, but they were few in number (nine, as against 209 bullheads), and the perch and sunfish he caught were comparable to the bullheads in their stuntedness and (to humans) worthlessness.

In the lower lake Trembley found much the same story, though in less exaggerated form. Small-mouth black bass were not yet extinct there, and most of the other species were less stunted than in the upper lake. But the difference was one of degree only, and it seemed clear that the lower lake was fast following the upper, which it resembles, into decline.

Trembley tested the lakes' waters chemically and found them very lacking in those minerals that nourish the microscopic organisms on which all other lake-life, ultimately, feeds. The lakes also—being on a plateau and draining only a small woodland area—have relatively few land-begotten nutrients washing into them. Thus they cannot support a luxuriant plant or fish population, and have presumably never done so: they are fated to be clear, rocky, sparsely inhabited "small-mouth bass lakes," in the phrase of the experts. This was fine in the old days, when the fishing pressure on them was light; but more recently, under heavier pressure, the lakes' systems have gone out of "balance." The life in a lake can be viewed as a pyramid. At its base is a mass of nutrients, either washed down from the land or generated in the water itself. Then comes a level of one-celled organisms, called plankton, which live off the nutrients, with or without the help of photosynthesis. Then come smaller masses of more complex organisms, which feed on those below them and in turn are fed on by those above. So it goes, up through insects, crayfish, minnows, etc.— larger beings eating smaller—to the pyramid's apex, which in my boyhood consisted of the bigger bass and pickerel. These big fish, their numbers not seriously threatened by the angling of those days, preyed heavily on the bullheads, sunfish, and small perch, keeping their populations in check; and this was proper "balance." But now the big bass are gone, or going, and the big pickerel are nearly so; and as a result the perch, sunfish, and bullheads have proliferated beyond all reason.

It is axiomatic among aquatic biologists, I have learned, that a given amount of food in a lake will support a fixed poundage of fish—either a great many little ones or a smaller number of fair-sized ones—and that once the little ones come to dominate, it is hard to reverse the trend. The Riga bass may have been hit by a tapeworm that is notorious in Connecticut waters and that can, if established, stop the species from reproducing. But this is not certain, and meanwhile we know that modern technology has taken a heavy toll of bass and pickerel both—by transporting an ever-increasing number of anglers to Mount Riga, and also by equipping them with fancy plugs and other lures that attract big predator-fish but not the smaller ones that formerly were caught as well. The fishing has grown so bad on Mount Riga that few serious fishermen go there now in summertime, but many still go for ice-fishing in the late fall and winter, when big pickerel—which do not go dormant then, like most other species, but roam hungrily about—are especially vulnerable; perhaps most of the lake's big pickerel are cleaned out annually this way, and the balance is kept permanently wrong. Some experts think that a series of closed winter seasons is the only way to restore it. Trembley has also suggested that numbers of the smaller fish be removed, and that nutrients be increased by manuring the lakes (in the past, it is thought, our lakes got more nutrients than now from manuring by wildfowl, which were more abundant). On Trembley's advice this last was tried some years ago on the lower lake; chicken-manure was spread on the ice there one winter, to sink and be absorbed in the spring. But the experiment wasn't made again—perhaps the effort was too great, perhaps the owners didn't like swimming in waters so treated. Nor are Trembley's other suggestions being tried; both Riga lakes are being let go, for the moment anyway, as unpromising for fish "management" (which in this case would have to be done, anyway, by the owners themselves, instead of the state, because the public's legal access rights are limited).

Last summer I went boating on both Riga lakes. It was July, and they were beautiful: blue water surrounded by green woods coming down to a rocky shore. In places the trees were dark hemlocks, in places they were lighter birches or maples or red oaks. They were never tall, for the soil is so shallow and poor on the plateau; looking at the woods now, I could see how they might supply few nutrients. In some places low laurel grew on the shore as well—hanging out over the water—and it was still in bloom then: pink and white blossoms amid the dark-green leaves, sometimes with a bumblebee humming above them. The rocks were gray clifflike ledges or big gray broken fragments. They came to the water's edge and sank below it, with little change beyond the addition of a faint slime of vegetation; a few yards off shore I looked down through clear water at the same big rock fragments, forming the bottom, and their grayness was only slightly greener. It was not *all* barren, though. Once I saw blue irises growing from the shallows, and in both lakes I found beds of water-lilies. The richest was near the inlet of the upper lake, where its main source-brook enters. There was a fair supply of nutrients there, apparently, and also of mud and silt, and these supported scattered lilies—often with films of green algae round their stalks—as well as a continuous coat of bottom-weeds, but short and sparse ones: nothing that could, by any licence, be called a tangle.

Two or three times, in the lakes, I saw schools of small fish darting along the bare rocks, but whether they were perch, sunfish, or what I could not tell. Once too I met a boatload of anglers, ranging in age from about five years to fifty. They were trolling desultorily in the lower lake, and they told me they had caught one little pickerel and several tiny perch and sunfish, all of which they had thrown back. They seemed bored, to say the least; they seemed to be fishing as a last resort.

Also last summer, on a Sunday morning, I went out briefly on West Twin Lake—of the shallow, weedy, mud-bound type—in a boat belonging to the late D. V. Garstin, a neighbor who lived near its shore. The lake has a much denser fish population than the Riga ones, and even before getting into the boat I saw schools of "blue-gill" sunfish swimming idly near the Garstins' dock, as if in an aquarium. Out on the lake I saw a dozen boats with fishermen; I assumed that most of these men had come by car from some distance—from the larger Connecticut towns like Torrington and Waterbury, for that is the rule here now. Some were fishing quietly with bait, others were casting plugs—hurling the plugs far out, with a sing of their reels, letting them plop in the water, then retrieving them slowly. This implied that they were after bass or pickerel, and I suppose catching

them reasonably often, though the only man I questioned said he was "getting nothing but small bluegills."
Perhaps he was being modest (thought good luck by
some fishermen), or perhaps he was telling the truth. I
have since learned that West Twin Lake—for reasons
I shall go into later—*has* got a stunted over-population
of bluegills, though otherwise it is said to be in excellent
balance; it yields a fine yearly crop of pickerel and large-
mouth bass, which are bigger, for their age, than the
Connecticut average.

West Twin Lake has a Chinese-landscape quality,
thanks partly to a small island: a rock with a single tree
rising decoratively from its side. Below the lake's surface
is a riot of green weeds, into which one can see for only
a few feet. As a boy I swam and waded in that lake, and
now I could remember it: remember my feet sinking
into the lukewarm ooze, remember the weeds clinging to
my ankles, raspingly. My brothers and I used to spend
nights with some contemporaries, the Pearce boys, in a
cabin they had on the shore. They had a home-made
aquaplane—a small board platform—that they towed
behind a boat with an outboard motor. You could sink
the prow of this aquaplane, in the clearer parts of the
lake, and make it dive and travel under water, down in
the weedy world. It was very green down there and you
could stay submerged until your breath gave out; once
one of us caught a turtle, by hand, while so diving. Indeed the lake was almost fetidly rich with life, and it
still is; and so are Long Pond (Wononpakook) and many
smaller ponds of that type in the township. From my
investigations I have learned that these waters usually
get lots of nutrients from nearby farms; that they are
shallow and hence permeated by sunlight and photosyn-

thesis; and that as a result they are warm-water jungles, bursting with plankton, weeds, bugs, grubs, fishes, and other creatures.

In the mid-'thirties I learned something about the smaller weed-ponds here. I was working in New York then, and coming to Salisbury for weekends. I had acquired notions of "sportsmanship"—now I might call it "snobbishness"—in fishing, which impelled me to use only artificial lures; in the springs I did endless fly-fishing, for trout, in the streams, and in the summers I varied this by plug-fishing, for bass and pickerel, in the weed-ponds. One place where my brothers and I used to go was a little pond near the Housatonic River; it was, I think, a former part of the Housatonic's course, long bypassed and dammed off. A barnyard drained into it, and it was warm, shallow, green, and very rich. We would sit in a boat on it and cast plugs toward the lily-pads round its edges, which were never far away. Often our plugs would foul in weeds as we reeled them in, but sometimes they would raise a good bass or pickerel, with a startling splash, amid the greenery. Small as the pond was, it seemed always to have its complement of predators.

Those bass were large-mouth. Small-mouth bass favored the rocky lakes, large-mouth the weedy ones; the two species were hard to tell apart, except by minute facial details, though I always felt that the large-mouth had a more greenish-black color to their deep bodies (the small-mouth being more brownish-black). As for the pickerel, they were long and very green, with yellow mottlings. All three fish were magnificent, the kings of our still waters. It never occurred to me, then, that they were not indigenous; I assumed that they had been in our lakes and ponds forever. But recently I have learned that small-mouth bass were introduced to Connecticut, after the coming of the white man, from more northerly waters like the Saint Lawrence and the Finger Lakes; whereas large-mouth were introduced from warmer, more southerly ones down toward Dixie. I have further learned, while reading up on local history, that pickerel too were introduced to at least some of our waters— though perhaps from others very nearby—in the early nineteenth century. Thus long before my boyhood, even, our town's fish ecology had been made artificial. This had been done in an amateurish way; various enthusiasts—on the order, no doubt, of Judge Warner—had thought that the fish of such-and-such a lake would do well in such-and-such another lake, and had transferred a few pails of them by buckboard or other primitive means. I myself, indeed, took part in such a transplanting as a boy; my father's farm had a shallow pond, not much bigger than a tennis court, and one summer we put a pailful of smallish Mount Riga bullheads in it. They didn't survive, so far as we could ever learn; perhaps they starved, perhaps they were cleaned out by snapping turtles that lived there (once, I remember, a man on our farm got one of these turtles to fasten on a pitchfork-handle and carried it home that way, for decapitation). If the bullheads *had* survived, they would now be part of the pond's fauna, and seemingly a primordial part to any newcomer who didn't know the history. That is how most of our lakes and ponds got their populations: through amateurish crisscrossing of the species by local men. "Fish management," the art or science of the professional biologists, was barely coming on the scene in the mid-'thirties.

Even today Connecticut fish management (I have been learning) doesn't concern itself much with the stocking of warm-water varieties: i.e. bass and pickerel and their "forage" fishes, or pyramidal supports, like perch, sunfish, and bullheads. These warm-water fish are all very prolific, the biologists say; once present in a suitable lake, they will do well unless the lake goes out of balance, a malady for which more stocking is not the answer. "If you have to stock warm-water fish," one biologist has told me, "there is something wrong with the lake, and you should cure it by some other method like closed seasons." (When I was a boy the stunting of fish was popularly blamed on inbreeding, for which new stocking was naturally thought a remedy, but today the biologists say this is rubbish; they say that stunting comes from over-population, which further stocking can only aggravate.)

Non-Connecticut fish management, it should be said, still does concern itself a lot with warm-water varieties, notably in Southern states like Alabama. In Alabama, in the 1930s, two biologists named Swingle and Smith learned that good fishing could be provided by the planned stocking of large-mouth bass along with bluegills as a forage fish; these two species combined with smaller organisms in successful pyramids that were often helped artificially, at the base, by the addition of fertilizer-nutrients to the water. The formula became famous in the South, and it has been tried in the North as well, but it hasn't transferred readily. Bluegills (they are blue-tinged members of the squarish sunfish tribe) are so prolific that the bass and pickerel in a lake, by themselves, cannot keep them down to reasonable numbers; they need the help of nearby humans, who must be willing to catch many bluegills, which they can then consume as "panfish," or small, inelegant frying fare. Southern humans, it seems, are ready to do this—in enough volume to keep the balance right—but Northern ones, nowadays, are not. In Salisbury a few Raggies do catch bluegills copiously in West Twin Lake and treat them as food; one Raggy sometimes gives a mess of them to my brother Jake, who has helped him in the past with legal problems. But men like that are getting scarce here. Most anglers who fish in Salisbury today—caught up in the new affluent world of fancy lures and "gourmet" foods—hold the bluegill in contempt as fare and quarry both. And that, presumably, is why the bluegills of West Twin Lake are so many and so small now.

Their over-population is seen as a problem by the Connecticut biologists, but as too slight a one to demand much action on their part. The biologists are investing little effort in West Twin Lake or our other weed-ponds —feeling that nature should take its course in them— just as they are investing nothing in the Riga lakes, because they are so unpromising (as well as being privately owned).

What they *are* investing in, and heavily, is the lakes of our third type, namely Lakeville Lake (Wononscopomuc) and East Twin, which are deep and cool enough to harbor trout and salmon. The culture of such fish—the *salmonidae*—has become almost the be-all and end-all of professional management in our lakes. This development was already under way in the 'thirties, though I was not aware of it then. What I *was* aware of, inevitably, was the heavy state stocking of trout in our streams, from the mighty Housatonic down to brooks that one could step across. Brook, brown, and rainbow trout were stocked in the streams on virtually a "put-and-take" basis, meaning that what was put in by the state was almost immediately taken out by the anglers; one commonly heard then that anglers followed the hatchery trucks to the very stream-banks, so the take would be as fast as possible. I suppose this closeness of fishing to stocking left little room for further development; I suppose that as the fishing pressure increased in Salisbury—which it has done many times over since the 'thirties—the state's managerial effort—also increasing many times over—needed new fields to work in, and the deep lakes provided them.*

Even before the 'thirties—my time of learning about stream-fish—I was aware that huge, mysterious lake trout existed in Lakeville Lake. Of course I thought they had been there forever—since God created the waters themselves—but I have since learned that they too had been introduced to Salisbury by man, like the bass; they had been brought here around 1900 from the Great Lakes or other big northern waters. I never saw one of these lake trout—I only heard about them—and they were not boy-quarry at all; they were for single-minded men who could troll patiently day after day, very deep, with hundreds of feet of heavy copper line. Lakeville Lake was supposed then to have a huge canyon in its bottom; in my imagination this place was murky and Wagnerian, and the big fish lurked in its caves and crenellations, waiting to strike—once in a great while— at some spoon that came dimly twinkling by on a copper line's end. Actually, of course, there was no canyon; the biologists, who have been de-mystifying our waters a

* See Chapter III for more about trout in streams.

good deal, have sounded Lakeville Lake scientifically
and found no great irregularity in its bottom, though
they have found considerable depth there: a hundred
and eight feet out near the middle. They have also
sounded most other Connecticut lakes, including East
Twin, where they have found a depth of eighty feet.
Lakeville Lake and East Twin are, it seems, among the
prime examples in Connecticut of "stratified" deep-
water lakes, or ones whose waters divide, as the summer
approaches, into layers of different temperature. The
waters of our shallower lakes don't do this; they are
mixed completely, by wind action, all summer long. The
deeper lakes are mixed completely, too, for a few weeks
in springtime, right after the ice melts; but soon their
colder waters sink down deep, their warmer ones rise,
and the wind cannot overcome this effect of gravity. A
stratified lake in summer is a three-layered sandwich. At
the top is what the biologists call the "epilimnion," a
warm-water layer of twenty feet or so; this is constantly
mixed by the wind and is much like the water in our
shallow, warmer lakes. Beneath it is another layer, the
"thermocline," of rapid temperature transition, and then
at the bottom is a static, never-warming "hypolimnion."
The waters of East Twin Lake were tested one September
recently, and the epilimnion was found to be over sev-
enty degrees Fahrenheit throughout, while the hypolimnion was under fifty. Trout and salmon like cool water,
and in Salisbury they cannot live the summer out in a
shallow lake or the epilimnion of a deep one. But in a
deep one they can retreat to the thermocline or hypolimnion and be comfortable. The hypolimnia of both our
deep lakes have plenty of dissolved oxygen, the biologists say, plus a good supply of zooplankton—one-celled

animal organisms—and of grubs, of little fish, and of
similar foods (they are more lacking in phytoplankton
—one-celled *plant* organisms—and in rooted vegetation,
because sunlight and photosynthesis fade out in the
depths). Trout and salmon can stay in the hypolimnia
of Lakeville Lake and East Twin indefinitely, getting
enough to eat and breathe, and hordes of them do so
through the warm season.

(A note on the nomenclature of our lakes may be in
order. "Wononscopomuc," an Indian name of doubtful
authenticity and unknown meaning, is applied to Lakeville Lake in maps, deeds, and other documents, and even
in the speech of certain more bookish humans, like some
of the Hotchkiss School boys whose campus overlooks its
waters. But in the townspeople's own speech the name
"Lakeville Lake" is used invariably, however repeti-
tive or circular it may be. Similarly "Wononpakook" is
called "Long Pond" in speech, and the Twin Lakes are
called the Twin Lakes, though they too have question-
able Indian names: Washinee and Washining, which
may possibly have meant, according to one writer,
"Laughing Water" and "Smiling Water.")

As boys we were aware of the lake trout, in the depths
of Lakeville Lake, but we knew much more about the
warm-water fish in the epilimnia of that lake and East
Twin—especially in the shallows along their shores.
These fish were, and still are, very like those of our weed-
ponds. Only a few summers ago I watched my nephew
Curtis take an eleven-inch big-mouth bass from the shallows of East Twin Lake, and it seemed hardly different
from the old weed-pond days. I also have on hand a letter, written five years ago, from a local friend who is a
great fisherman, and this gives some idea of the deep-

lake warm-water fishing in our boyhood days and now
(my friend's life began a few years before mine and has
been largely spent in and near Lakeville Lake; he wrote
the letter in answer to my questions about changes, and
he asked me not to tell his name).

Here are my observations [he says] for what they may be
worth to you. Lakeville Lake (Wononscopomuc) used to have a
number of smallmouth black bass when I was a teenager (I
remember seeing some from 1920 to 1940). I can recall taking a
few of them, about a pound or better, on worms or live bait, such
as small shiners or frogs—we rarely caught any on plugs, etc.
There were many bigmouth bass, pickerel, perch, etc. too, but
only lake trout of the trout species. . . . There are still quite a
few bigmouth bass of good size (in the lake) and a number of
large pickerel (there don't seem to be as many smaller bass and
pickerel as there were formerly). I haven't seen a smallmouth
black bass in years in our lake. Of course there are the stocked
trout (brooks, browns, rainbows) and many . . . perch, blue-
gill sunfish, bullheads, suckers, etc. . . .

I can recall vividly how many bigmouth bass used to be taken
out of Lakeville Lake per day. We thought nothing of catching
half a dozen bass in a couple hours of plug casting or fishing
with bait. They would average anywhere from one and a half
to four pounds. I saw two that Clarence Bartholomew caught on
topwater plug about 1923, I think—one weighed nine pounds, the
other seven. Taken at night in Milmine's cove. . . .

Heroic as such fishing seemed to us, it doesn't greatly
interest the new fish biologists, who think Lakeville
Lake's resources are rather wasted on warm-water fish
and should be reserved for the *salmonidae*. Recently,
after beginning my lake investigations, I learned that
the State Fish and Game Commission had held hearings
in Salisbury, in the late 1950s, on the possibility of "reclaiming" Lakeville Lake to this end; "reclaiming" is a
fish-management euphemism for poisoning the fish out
of a lake and replacing them by a new, artificial population thought more desirable. I couldn't learn much

about these hearings in Salisbury itself—I got only vague, contradictory reports of them—but in time the matter was cleared up for me in Hartford, the state capital, by a Mr. Cole Wilde, a graduate biologist who heads the fish division of the State Fish and Game Commission and is thus the final Connecticut authority on the subject. I saw Mr. Wilde on April 12, just four days before the 1966 fishing season opened, and he was a busy man. Clean-shaven, bespectacled, and of medium age and height, he sat in his shirtsleeves at his Hartford desk, which was piled high with papers, and answered repeated phone calls in between explaining to me the subtleties of stocking, "reclamation," and other aspects of his art. He was on the phone several times about an unexplained "fish kill," or sudden wholesale death of fishes, on a stream north of Hartford. He received one call from a man complaining that a tree had been felled over a certain trout brook, and asking that it be removed. He received another asking why a state lobster hatchery, somewhere on Long Island Sound, had been abandoned, and still another inquiring about a fish-elevator that was being designed for getting shad over a new dam on the Farmington River. He handled all these matters with patience, clarity, and, when indicated, decisiveness. He told the tree-complainer that his men couldn't possibly clean up the mess (which he was sure they hadn't created) as they were all busy with pre-season stocking. He told the lobster-inquirer that the hatchery had been abandoned because it was accomplishing nothing. He told the elevator-inquirer about the project in great detail. And concerning the fish kill he arranged, by phone, to get one of his men onto the scene as soon as possible, there to take samples of the water and learn what he could of the kill's causes and implications. Mr. Wilde also kept the state's public-health people informed of his actions in this regard, by phone, since fish kills concern them too.

He did these things calmly and politely, like a very model of the technological administrator, and meanwhile he told me about fish management. First he said that Connecticut *does* engage in some warm-water management, though on a minor scale and hardly at all in Salisbury itself. "One thing we do," he said, "is to lower the levels of certain lakes in order to keep them in balance. If you draw down a lake, which also lessens its area, you concentrate the fish population, and the predators have a better chance to work on the forage fish; the latter have less space to run or hide in, so in a few months the predators get their numbers down to size. The outlets of many Connecticut lakes were dammed up long ago— say in the nineteenth century—as a way of raising the level and getting more power for small industries. The water was manipulated by use of the dams—let out in the summer, usually, when it was scarce, and allowed to rise again in the winter—and we believe this seasonal level-changing had a good effect, unintentionally, on the fish populations. Now those small industries are nearly all gone, of course, but we still use the dams of some lakes for level-changing in fish management. Unfortunately the summer is the best time to draw down a lake, for our purposes, and that is when its waters are in most demand for recreation. It is hard to convince a shore-owner that the water should be drawn down when he wants to swim in it, and so we usually do it in the fall. We don't do it to any Salisbury lake, it happens, but we do, for instance, annually draw down Wood Creek

Pond in Norfolk, which is near there. The state owns the shores of Wood Creek Pond, and that makes it easier."

Another device in warm-water management is "partial reclamation." Fish can be poisoned selectively, Mr. Wilde explained, to some extent. There is a way of poisoning bluegills, for instance, that greatly reduces their numbers while killing only a few of the bass and other fish in the same water. This has been used on some Connecticut lakes—ones where the dead bluegills were not expected to be objectionable—though there is no plan for trying it on West Twin. "Some warm-water lakes have too many species for successful management," Mr. Wilde said. "It is too hard to foresee all the possibilities. You do something to help one species, and it helps another instead. Or it hurts two or three species, unexpectedly, that you don't want to hurt. For warm-water management you should have a lake with only two or three species, but such lakes are rare in Connecticut. From the late nineteenth century up into the 1930s there was indiscriminate stocking, of many varieties, in most of our lakes, and this has left chaotic populations that are hard to manage."

Fifteen or more varieties have been stocked in Lakeville Lake in the past, Mr. Wilde said, but no warm-water fish have been added (with the state's knowledge, at least) since the 1930s, a time when the scientific stocking of *salmonidae* was getting under way there. "Lakeville Lake is exceptionally good trout water," he said, "and we have superb growth records for trout stocked in it. Since the 'thirties, therefore, we have been managing it for trout primarily. In the late 'fifties we felt we should reclaim it, if possible, and mange it exclusively for one variety: for rainbow trout, which we would stock annually as fingerlings—an inch or two long—and which would feed entirely on plankton; the lake would have no forage fish under this plan—no fish of any kind but the rainbows themselves. Rainbows are great plankton eaters. They don't grow very big on it; I imagine they just can't get enough of it for that, even by swimming around all the time with their mouths open. The lake would not yield trophy fish with this kind of management, but it would yield a great many between ten and fourteen inches long; we have estimated an annual harvest of fifty thousand such fish, as against ten thousand fish with the existing balance. The method would be cheap, too, as we would be stocking fingerlings—there being no predators to kill them off. We would have to stock each year, as rainbows don't reproduce in Lakeville Lake—they run up streams to spawn, and the lake has no suitable one flowing into it—but we can raise fingerlings cheaply enough, from eggs, in our hatcheries. We have tested this kind of management a good deal in other waters. In Ball Pond in Fairfield, for instance, we stock fingerling rainbows each year on May 15, and they are eleven or twelve inches long by the opening day of the next season. Ball Pond is public water, which raises problems for management; in such waters someone always puts a pailful of another variety, or several other varieties, back in soon. Then the population gets complicated, and we have to reclaim again; we reclaim Ball Pond about every four years. This isn't necessary with well-controlled waters, as we have shown at Doolittle Pond in Norfolk. Doolittle is owned by a club and tightly supervised. The club began managing for rainbows eight years ago, at its own expense, and the lake still has a pure rainbow population that gives excellent fishing. So we think that form of management is good if the neighborhood is educated up to it."

As for the hearings on reclaiming Lakeville Lake, these had not been required by law, I learned, but had been a matter of policy. "We don't like to reclaim a lake if there is much opposition," Mr. Wilde said, "because then people put the old varieties back in immediately, and our work is wasted." The Lakeville hearings revealed a great deal of such opposition, though the reasons are rather obscure by now. I believe some citizens hated the thought of losing the bass and pickerel. Others no doubt wanted their children to catch sunfish off the docks as they had done. Others may have recoiled at the idea of poisoning, or of dead fish floating about, or just of creeping socialism in general. Anyway there were many objections, and the state backed off. "We let it drop," Mr. Wilde told me. "Some day, when the people know more about it, they may want us to come in and manage for rainbow, and then we'll do it. But we are not pushing the idea."

As an alternative, soon after the Lakeville Lake hearings, the state decided to stock alewives and thus commit itself to a different management formula, which still prevails. "Alewives are originally salt-water herring," Mr. Wilde explained, "but they have become landlocked in some Connecticut waters by the building of dams. They grow to about six inches, they do very well in the depths of stratified lakes, and we stock them as forage fish for trout. Brown trout, a species we want to encourage anyway, do especially well on them. In 1953 we ran a creel census of Lakeville Lake, financed under the Federal Aid to Fisheries Act. We stocked numbers of brown, brook, and rainbow trout—the three most popular species—at several different times, with the fish marked differently each time by either tagging or fin-clipping. Then our men kept a careful record of the anglers' catch of these fish. We collected a mass of data, and from it concluded that brown trout yielded much the best fishing per dollar of investment—I am talking now, you understand, of a mixed population in the lake, not a pure one of plankton-eating rainbows. *Some* rainbows are desirable in a mixed lake too, we concluded in '53, because they give good fishing in the late summer and fall, which the browns don't—browns are spring fish primarily. After the creel census we recommended that stockings of seventy-five per cent brown trout and twenty-five per cent rainbows would be advisable in Lakeville Lake. So browns are the main thing, you see, and they do grow very fast on ale-wives. Not all of them switch over to alewives, incidentally. Small browns live on plankton and other minute forage, then later most switch to alewives but some don't, and you can see the difference between the two. If they stay off alewives they remain slimmer and keep the usual brown-trout colors, a yellowish golden-brown with bright red spots. If they go on alewives they grow bigger and stockier and turn silvery like Atlantic salmon. They grow very fast. If a brown trout in Lakeville Lake escapes the anglers it will grow from half a pound to five pounds, on alewives, in two years. Many trophy browns, there-fore, have been caught in Lakeville Lake recently. Last year a nine-pound one was caught, as I remember it, and perhaps some bigger ones. And we know from netting that there are twelve- and thirteen-pounders in the lake. The big ones are hard to catch—you must troll for them down around thirty-five feet—but they are there, and we are trying to encourage that high-survival type. Recently we netted a female brown in Lakeville Lake that we had stocked six years earlier and that weighed eleven pounds. We are breeding from her and hope to develop a longer-living, bigger-growing strain thereby.

"This year, too, we are trying an experiment in Lakeville Lake with Kamloops trout, a variety of rainbow; we hope they will learn to eat alewives, as our other rainbows don't, and grow to trophy sizes. Early in March we planted 2000 yearling Kamloops, averaging nearly a foot long, which had been raised in our hatcheries from Pacific Northwest eggs. In the Northwest, their native habitat, the Kamloops can be voracious fish-eaters. In Lake Pend Oreille in Idaho they feed on small Kokanee salmon and grow to thirty pounds or more; the record Kamloops ever caught, from Lake Pend Oreille, was something like thirty-seven pounds. We don't expect quite that in Lakeville Lake, but if the Kamloops will eat alewives we hope they will produce trophy fish on a par with the browns. Rainbows are more spectacular to catch than browns—they do more jumping and so on—and perhaps the Kamloops will make a nice variation. If they do well we can stock more in the future."

I asked about East Twin and found that despite its similarity to Lakeville Lake, in depth and stratification, it is being managed quite differently. "For one thing," Mr. Wilde said, "we have never considered reclaiming it for rainbows. It is not tight enough to reclaim. It has substantial streams draining into it, which would have to be reclaimed at the same time, very thoroughly, and it is connected by a channel to West Twin, which is a natural for warm-water varieties and should be left that way. East Twin itself has good warm-water fishing, which shouldn't be disturbed either. Lakeville Lake is a tight

package, without important tributaries or other compli-
cations, and is suitable for reclamation as East Twin is
not.

"Secondly, while there are brown trout in East Twin,
they do not usually grow to trophy size, like those in
Lakeville Lake, because they have no alewives to feed
on. We keep alewives out of East Twin because they are
plankton-eaters and would compete with sockeye salmon,
a species that likewise lives on plankton and that has become the lake's leading game fish. Sockeyes were mys-
teriously found spawning in a shallow part of East Twin
in the 'thirties. No one knew how they had got there,
though if you asked around now you might find fifty
people who would claim to have put them in. Anyway
that population died out by the late 'thirties, and the
state put sockeyes in again, produced from British Co-
lumbia eggs; the sockeye too is a Northwest fish. Now we
stock them annually; they can spawn in the lake, in that
one shallow place, but few mature fish result from this.
Every year, therefore, we net and squeeze some East
Twin sockeyes in October, their spawning time, and take
the eggs to our hatchery at Burlington, near Torrington.
The eggs hatch into fry, and we put these back in—not
only into East Twin, but into five other Connecticut lakes
as well. The program costs about a thousand dollars a
year for all six lakes, which is very cheap. We can put
the sockeyes in as fry because they go deeper down than
little trout and thus escape the warm-water predators,
the bass and pickerel. The big sockeyes don't eat the little
ones either, as would be the case with *Atlantic* salmon.
They stick to plankton, in which East Twin is exceptionally rich; it has a large drainage area, with many nutrients washing down from farms. The sockeye fishing gets

better every year in East Twin, and nowadays a number of three-and-a-half pound fish are caught. They are pretty deep down, and fishermen must troll for them with copper or lead-centered line, which hinders their fighting when they are hooked. But still they are a good game fish, and for the present we don't see how the East Twin balance can be improved on. That is why we don't stock alewives and try for trophy browns, as in Lakeville Lake."

I asked about the lake trout in Lakeville Lake, and Mr. Wilde said they were still around. "The population is hanging on," he said, "though no additions have been stocked for years. The yield isn't good enough; the lake can't support really fishable numbers. Lake trout are very carnivorous; they are the top of their food chain—the apex of their pyramid—like muskellunge in the northern lakes or tigers in the jungle. It takes a lot of water to feed each fish, and so they are spaced far apart —say one or two to the acre, and that down deep where the acres are fewer. We know there are thirty-pound trout in Lakeville Lake because our men have netted them when checking. Last year someone caught a six-teen-pounder too, but that was exceptional. Only one or two lake trout are caught a year now, and if we re-claimed the lake that would be the end of them."

That was the end of my researches, too, into the higher abstractions of fish management, except that I did pay a visit to the Burlington hatchery, which is twenty-odd miles southeast of Salisbury. The hatchery was big and barnlike, standing by a brook between grassy fields and hemlocks. Along the brook, out in the open, were many round ponds containing trout of different sizes. Inside the building, amid a constant splash and gurgle of falling water, were many long concrete tanks, some containing other mature fish, some fingerlings or fry (and there was a big closet, too, with fresh-watered trays of eggs in it). The tanks were labeled, and the names gave a feeling of the *salmonidae*'s variety and cosmopolitanism. BROOK TROUT, they said, RAINBOW TROUT, SOCKEYE SALMON, PLYMOUTH BROWN, LAKEVILLE BROWN, ENGLISH BROWN, LAKE TROUT, SWEDEN BROWN, DANISH BURL, WESTERN BROWN. The Lakeville browns, I learned from men in attendance there, were progeny of the eleven-pound female Mr. Wilde had told me about. The Plymouth browns were a hatchery-bred strain, already developed for a few generations—by natural selection under these artificial conditions—to grow well in the tanks and to be caught easily enough, on a put-and-take basis, when stocked. (The state was breeding in two directions, in other words—toward good survival and trophy sizes, with the Lakeville browns, and toward non-survival or quick return, with the Plymouth.) The other tank-labels stood for *salmonidae* of more natural variations. Brook trout are the indigenous *salmonidae* of eastern North America: the speckled natives that the colonists found in our streams. Brown trout are European *salmonidae*, essentially; rainbows are western North American ones; and so on. Through past ages the *salmonidae* have spread over the Northern Hemisphere and developed their variations. Some have come to migrate tiny distances, in fresh water only, for their spawning; others have come to migrate vast ones, through fresh and salt water both. Some, like the Atlantic salmon, have come to spawn several times in their lives; others, like the Pacific salmon, to spawn only once and die. Some have come to be brown, some to have pink rainbow stripes, some to be silvery. The twentieth century has found them in place in their infinite variety—in Siberia, the Pacific, Canada, the Atlantic, Scandinavia, wherever—and has begun, by technology, to move them about and scramble them. Thus they have been gathered, in places like this Burlington hatchery, in almost UN or NATO fashion. They have become the main chess-pieces of fresh-water management, and as such I saw them lying there now, awaiting the biologists' inspirations.

I walked among the tanks. Some had big fish, lying deep in them, like dark and streamlined stones. Others had fingerlings with thin wedge bodies—accent-shaped —stippling the water in depth. Others had fry, and these were tiny; when one darted through a tank it looked not like an entity, but a black jiggly line. I went outdoors, and the round pools lay warming in the sunshine. Some had foot-long trout in them, some smaller ones. A few of the trout jumped, some glided, but most just lay there, basking. They were a dark khaki, lying over sandy, lighter-khaki ground. In the round pools they lay in concentric circles, nose to tail—round and round, circle within circle, like Van Gogh's suns. They lay there waiting, for what they did not know.

I left the hatchery, and soon afterward, on April 16, I went to the season's opening at Lakeville Lake. Since my boyhood, I had heard, the event had taken on a saturnalian quality, of a big mass festival. I was curious about this, naturally, and in the end I wasn't disappointed. I approached the lake at a quarter to five that morning— it was light by then—and found seventeen cars lined up at a gate there, though the opening hour was not till six.

A few of the cars had boats on trailers behind them, a few had boats upside down on their roofs. I parked my own car, some distance off, and walked past the gate to the lake. Most of that lake's shore is privately owned, and public access is only at this one point, of my approach. The spot has been greatly developed since my boyhood, like so many other things. There used to be a simple oak-grove there, and a shantylike building where a man named Dave Timmins kept a small boat-livery and tackle shop. Now the grove has been turned into a real town park, with benches and tables and a big recreation building; and the shanty has solidified into something more municipal—supervised by an able public servant, Frank Markey, who keeps assistants and handles many times the old volume of business. He keeps a few dozen boats there too, for rent, and he had earlier told me that these had been booked long ago—since January 19—for the opening. They lay there now, tied to docks, and out beyond them some other, private, boats rode at anchor. Fishermen were moving to the boats already; and soon, when the gate had opened, other fishermen drove in and launched their own. They backed their trailers to the beach and slid the boats off.

The Lakeville Girl Scouts, as part of the new festivities, have taken to serving breakfast, for money, in the big recreation building. They begin at five a.m., I had heard, and so at five I went there. I found them selling orange juice, coffee, scrambled eggs, sausages, doughnuts, and cinnamon buns. They had a blazing fire going, too, in a fireplace, and I ate a big breakfast and warmed myself. The recreation building had plate-glass windows, and through these I could see the lake between the big old oak trees; the trees were bare except for a few brown leaves from autumn. Between the trunks the lake showed gray, reflecting a gray sky, and around its shore were dotted houses amid bits of woodland, these also mainly brown now. The lake was still, like a mirror, and a faint mist rose from it. Birds were singing when I went outdoors again; near the water I heard the buzzing trill of redwings.

The lakeshore was getting busier all the time now, with men arriving and climbing into boats—two men, usually, in each—and then deploying out onto the lake, to be in favored spots by six. The men wore rough clothes, often with red touches; and most of them, I gathered, had come from far away. "They come from Bridgeport, Stamford, everywhere," a local friend I met there said. "It's a big event, all right." And he shook his head.

I found myself conversing with a lady there, who said she lived by the lake, in a cottage, and had three children between ten and sixteen. I asked her what she thought of the "reclamation" proposal, and she said she didn't like it. "My children catch perch and panfish in the lake," she said. "I make them clean and scale the fish themselves, and I cook them and we eat them. It is good that way. The lake has all kinds of things in it. There are snapping turtles, you know, and in one place there is a big mama bass—people dive down to the mama bass and tickle her, and she just lies there. That is how the lake should be. We would hate to see it changed."

Six o'clock came and went, and by six-twenty the first pair of anglers had caught their limit, of five fish each. They brought them ashore, and Frank Markey pointed them out to me. The fish were beauties, by the standards of my childhood: browns and rainbows running to twelve or fourteen inches. The browns *were* silvery, I saw; they were silver-sided, and their spots were not bright red, but dark. The rainbows were silvery too, as they normally are, with lovely pink stripes down their sides. (Some may have been the newly stocked Kamloops; I don't know.)

Some little boys, I suddenly noticed, were getting their limits too, of nice-looking browns, in a pond by the lake's outlet. The lake had a dam there, from the old industrial days, and below this lay the pond, a small one with grassy banks. The pond was almost bursting with fish, I soon decided, and I went and questioned Frank, who told me three hundred had been stocked in it the week before; only children twelve and under, he said, were allowed to catch them. The children were fishing in a good old-fashioned way, with worms and sinkers and bobbers. They were hauling in the brown trout—which were really brown and up to a foot in length—and letting them flop about there, on the grass. The scene was like a concept of boy-paradise.

I left the shore, went back to my car, and drove off to East Twin Lake, a trip of fifteen minutes. I went to O'Hara's, a commercial boat-livery there that is the center for out-of-town fishermen. The lake was densely speckled with boats, I noted—at least as densely as Lakeville Lake, which is saying a lot—but no one was catching much. It was too early for the sockeye salmon, I was told at O'Hara's—they would be readier in a month or two—and the lake's trout, for some reason, had not begun biting at that hour.

I went back to Lakeville Lake, but not to the grove immediately. Instead I went to see a neighbor, Tom

Wagner, a Lakeville lawyer, who has a cabin elsewhere on the shore and who entertains his male friends and acquaintances there on the opening weekend. This function has grown up through the years, I understand; but to me it was pure innovation, and I linked it, like the doings at the grove, with the new big-time era of local fishing. The Wagner camp was a modest frame one, it turned out, down on the lake behind the Wagner house; there was a flagstone terrace there; a big barbecue with a chimney; two or three sturdy tables; and plenty of chairs, crockery, cutlery, coffee-pots, bottles, and so on. And in the air were smells of coffee and bacon.

Five or six men were on hand, some of them just in from fishing, and they too had been doing well. One of them, Russell Ottey—a near neighbor of the Wagners and an expert angler—showed me a mess he had caught; they were in the water, tied by a line through their gills to the dock. Again they were nice browns and rainbows, running up to fourteen inches. Mr. Ottey had caught them, he said, on "hardware," meaning a small spoon or spinner cast and retrieved just below the surface. That was the level at which trout were being taken, I gathered, now in this cool season. All over the lake they were taken a few inches down, on hardware or, less often, on wet flies.

I sat drinking coffee and enjoying the scene. I heard a wild goose honking, and I listened to the men talk. They were local residents, or at least had local connections, and they took a dim view, I learned, of the mass of strangers on the lake, whom they referred to, collectively, as "Bridgeport and Waterbury."

The lake was teeming now with boats—moving about,

crossing each other's bows, weaving between each other like ducks on a crowded pond. One guest looked out at them. "I wonder how it is in Central Park today," he said disdainfully.

Tom Wagner, who lives in the camp all summer with his wife, told me that he habitually feeds bread then, every day, to the sunfish off his dock. "When I come out to feed them," he said, "they see the door of my screen porch opening, and they start for the dock. They come in swarming from all directions. Last summer, too, a pickerel used to lie under my canoe there, and when the sunfish came in, snap! he would get one every time."

This reminded me, somehow, of the mama bass that people tickled, and I asked Mr. Wagner what the community thought, in his opinion, of the idea of reclamation—of poisoning out the sunfish, the pickerel, and the other local color.

He thought a moment. "The community doesn't like it," he said. "They think the fish-and-game people don't know what they're doing. They'll clean out the fish that are here and put in trout so Bridgeport and Waterbury will come more and more. It won't do the local people any good, and they don't like it."

"Bridgeport and Waterbury will come more and more," another man said. "And the state will be stocking fish on Friday to be caught on Saturday and Sunday."

I left them, feeling I had dug down to a basic conflict. On one side were the local people; their rights and sentiments and traditions; and the "natural" order. On the other were Bridgeport and Waterbury; their taxes; their need for recreation; and the growing authority, in fish as in other fields, of technology and planning. The two seemed locked in combat. To me it was interesting, though I wasn't taking sides. Nor was I predicting the outcome, though I felt a guess was possible.

I went back to the grove, anyway, and Bridgeport and Waterbury were doing fine. Boat after boat was coming in, with fishermen who had caught their limit; Frank Markey later said a thousand trout were taken that day —no "trophy" ones, but big enough ones still: bigger, on the average, than in previous years, because of some mystery of stocking policy. So Bridgeport and Waterbury came ashore, with their catches. They hauled their boats out, onto their trailers, and drove away, leaving our township, temporarily, to its townsmen.